W9-CDX-025

"*Substantial Classrooms* is an engaging and inspiring look at an aspect of the educational system – substitute teaching – that has gone unexamined for too long. What if...? How might we...? These simple questions become decisive turning points in a book sparked by inspiration, fueled by empathy, and fortified by years of on-the-ground (in-the-schools) research. Amanda and Jill have not only done the work to prove you can jump in and turn small hacks into surprising, systemic change – they'll radically alter how you see substitute teaching."

—Arne Duncan, former US Secretary of Education

"After a career of leading work to develop and support teachers, *Substantial Classrooms* is the first book I've seen that takes an optimistic and practical look at how substitute teaching can be a positive, and integral, part of teaching our next generation. I can imagine that a lot of people will initially hesitate before cracking a book on subbing, but I can assure you, if you're looking for encouragement – and answers! – *Substantial Classrooms* is the place to start."

—Ellen Moir, Founder, New Teacher Center

"The *Substantial Classrooms* story is exactly the kind we hope for when we select d.school fellows. By effectively applying design thinking to the broad-spectrum educational challenges that surround substitute teaching, *Substantial Classrooms* is opening new pathways to collaboration, innovation, and truly significant change."

—David Kelley, Founder, IDEO and Stanford's Hasso Plattner Institute of Design (the d.school)

Substantial Classrooms

Substantial Classrooms

Redesigning the Substitute Teaching Experience

Jill Vialet & Amanda von Moos

ILLUSTRATIONS
BY
ABBY VANMUIJEN

JB JOSSEY-BASS™

A Wiley Brand

Copyright © 2021 by John Wiley & Sons, Inc. All rights reserved.

Published by Jossey-Bass
A Wiley Imprint
111 River St, Hoboken, NJ 07030
www.josseybass.com

No part of this publication may be reproduced, stored in a retrieval system, or transmitted in any form or by any means, electronic, mechanical, photocopying, recording, scanning, or otherwise, except as permitted under Section 107 or 108 of the 1976 United States Copyright Act, without either the prior written permission of the Publisher, or authorization through payment of the appropriate per-copy fee to the Copyright Clearance Center, Inc., 222 Rosewood Drive, Danvers, MA 01923, (978) 750–8400, fax (978) 646–8600, or on the Web at www.copyright.com. Requests to the Publisher for permission should be addressed to the Permissions Department, John Wiley & Sons, Inc., 111 River Street, Hoboken, NJ 07030, (201) 748–6011, fax (201) 748–6008, or online at http://www.wiley.com/go/permissions.

Limit of Liability/Disclaimer of Warranty: While the publisher and author have used their best efforts in preparing this book, they make no representations or warranties with respect to the accuracy or completeness of the contents of this book and specifically disclaim any implied warranties of merchantability or fitness for a particular purpose. No warranty may be created or extended by sales representatives or written sales materials. The advice and strategies contained herein may not be suitable for your situation. You should consult with a professional where appropriate. Neither the publisher nor author shall be liable for any loss of profit or any other commercial damages, including but not limited to special, incidental, consequential, or other damages.

For general information on our other products and services or for technical support, please contact our Customer Care Department within the United States at (800) 762–2974, outside the United States at (317) 572–3993 or fax (317) 572–4002.

Wiley publishes in a variety of print and electronic formats and by print-on-demand. Some material included with standard print versions of this book may not be included in e-books or in print-on-demand. If this book refers to media such as a CD or DVD that is not included in the version you purchased, you may download this material at http://booksupport.wiley.com. For more information about Wiley products, visit www.wiley.com.

Library of Congress Cataloging-in-Publication Data:
Names: Vialet, Jill, author. | Moos, Amanda von, author.
Title: Substantial classrooms : redesigning the substitute teaching experience / Jill Vialet, Amanda von Moos.
Description: San-Francisco : Jossey-Bass, 2020. | Includes bibliographical references and index.
Identifiers: LCCN 2020010620 (print) | LCCN 2020010621 (ebook) | ISBN 9781119663652 (paperback) | ISBN 9781119663850 (adobe pdf) | ISBN 9781119663836 (epub)
Subjects: LCSH: Substitute teaching--United States. | Substitute teachers—United States. | Educational change—United States.
Classification: LCC LB2844.1.S8 V53 2020 (print) | LCC LB2844.1.S8 (ebook) | DDC 371.14/122—dc23
LC record available at https://lccn.loc.gov/2020010620
LC ebook record available at https://lccn.loc.gov/2020010621

COVER DESIGN & ART: PAUL MCCARTHY

SKY10025584_031221

This book is dedicated to
Cristin Quealy,
for all the things.

Table of Contents

Foreword

Back in 2007 when we first began to envision the K12 Lab at Stanford's Hasso Plattner Institute of Design (a.k.a. the d.school), we knew we wanted to create professional development experiences that inspired educators and set them on a journey to creatively engage with their students, content, school, and communities. We were fired up about the potential for using design thinking to activate students and teachers, but it wasn't entirely clear how we would go about it.

Fundamentally, we were inspired by the belief that humans are, by nature, designers. We define design as *creative problem solving and innovation*—so we could see immediately that educators design constantly. They (and likely you) design assignments, curriculum, assessments, interventions, rituals, spaces, processes, and, of course, work-arounds of innumerable varieties. As we explored our first prototype, crafting an Innovation Lab at a local school, we noticed one thing that particularly interested us: the teachers who truly embraced their designer identities were some of the most successful, both with students and in making change happen. They were ready, willing, and able to try things and learn from what didn't work. For them, prototyping and experimenting were power tools that did not require a power cord.

Through our early prototypes we understood that our special sauce was helping other players in the education sector make design experiments happen. From 2012 to 2017 we made that our overriding goal: Make Experiments Happen. We engaged in a huge number of experiments at all levels of the system. We worked with teachers, leaders, specialists, policy folks, technologists, entrepreneurs—a long and eclectic list of people interested in making positive change on some of the education system's most intractable problems. We also collaborated with like-minded organizations who wanted to take up our approach to design-focused experimentation. Through this work, we designed (and supported the design of) a diverse array of outputs: new school models, new consulting orgs, new professional development platforms, new classroom technologies, new curriculum for youth to explore their communities, and new frameworks for designing for racial equity, to name a few.

To help us do this work, we focused specifically on finding and supporting folks we like to call "edu innovators." These innovators were not necessarily classroom teachers, but rather entrepreneurially-minded catalysts who were seeing challenges in the field and wondering about how to address them. Their intention wasn't to make superficial change; they hoped to uproot systemic inequities. We were looking for folks who, if successful, might create big change. And we were looking for challenges that we could start to work on by using the tools of human-centered design.

Jill Vialet landed at the K12 Lab as an "edu fellow" because she was one of these leaders, and substitute teaching was a challenge that, when we heard her speak about it, left us speechless. How was it possible that within our education system there was a role merely titled "substitute?" Given the intriguing tentacles of the challenge—staffing, training, and profound equity implications—we thought it was exactly the kind of challenge that would benefit from a human-centered design approach.

In the book you hold in your hands, Jill and Amanda share the design journey that led them to create Substantial Classrooms and SubPlans. I am so pleased they have taken the time to share their journey with you. It sheds light on the specific challenge of substitute teaching, and also shows us the power of human-centered design to inspire an empathic lens, and a bias toward using experimentation to create change.

Their curiosity, commitment, and good humor in engaging in this work have been clear as long as I've known them, and these attributes shine through in this book—kind of amazing if you consider that it's a book about one of the most neglected and challenging aspects many systems face. Perhaps this is the book's greatest strength: while substitute teaching has been historically neglected and frustrating, Amanda and Jill have created a new, dynamic, positive narrative that flips the script.

Substantial demonstrates how the design framework offers a powerful model for reimagining aspects of our educational system that is both innovative and respectful, fundamentally acknowledging that the people in our educational communities—teachers, administrators, students, and families—are already in possession of the solutions we need.

My hope is that in reading this book, you will be able to see yourself in the ideas and innovators that Amanda and Jill describe, and that you will come away inspired to make a difference in the substitute teaching experience. Beyond that, I hope that following their journey will make you feel brave. Your work matters, and your empathic care and principled experimentation can contribute to change that can make a real difference for our next generation, especially in the lives of children who are furthest from opportunity. This book will help you think about making progress on your own challenges—with substitute teaching and beyond.

Susie Wise, PhD

Founder and Former Director, K12 Lab
Hasso Plattner Institute of Design
Stanford University

INTRODUCTION

NICE TO MEET YOU!

SUBSTITUTE TEACHING

THERE'S ROOM FOR HOPE

Substantial

This is a book about substitute teaching, but probably not the book you are expecting. While most of what is written about substitute teaching focuses on what subs can do to make the current system work better, this book invites you to both reconsider and redesign the system. You won't find tips and tricks for substitute teachers. Instead, we offer an understanding of how the system works today, an introduction to design thinking, and inspiring examples of people and places that are imagining a different future for substitute teaching. Most importantly, what you'll find here is an invitation to roll up your sleeves and join us in working to improve the substitute teaching experience—for everyone.

Substitute teaching is a more integral part of every student's education than most people realize. By the time our students graduate from high school, they will have spent a full year with substitute teachers. The experiences our students have with substitute teachers—substitute *learning* experiences—are decidedly mixed. Some days are great, others not so much. Today, almost nothing is done to ensure those days are set up for success.

It's time to change that.

Three years ago, we founded Substantial, a nonprofit that aims to bring more focus and intentional design to what happens when regular teachers are out of the classroom. We wrote this book to share what we've learned and to invite you to join us in this work.

We think that once you see the potential—and the current impact—of substitute teaching, it's hard to unsee it. But seeing the potential isn't enough. That's why we've paired this deep dive into the substitute teaching system with an introduction to design. When we launched Substantial we made a conscious decision to actively incorporate the design process and mindsets into the way we approach the work. In part, we hoped that the sizzle of design might rub off a bit on the fundamentally unsexy nature of substitute teaching, or that the unlikely pairing would be disarming enough to get people's attention. Mostly, though, we were just convinced that it works.

How We Got Here

To start, a little about how we came to work on substitute teaching. It's an unusual focus, and our paths to it were also a bit unusual. Amanda is a self-described improvement nerd—she lights up at the chance to make things work better and help people feel great about their work. She first started working on the substitute teaching issue when she was a principal coach for the Oakland Unified School District back in the mid-2000s. It was an issue that many of the schools she supported struggled with, and she spent many afternoons in human resources (HR) trying to troubleshoot on behalf of principals.

When she moved into the role of process improvement coach, working on those systems that had so vexed principals at the district level, substitute teaching was the focus of one of her first projects. At that point, one- third of the sub jobs in the district went unfilled, which was devastating to the schools that struggled the most to attract and retain subs. Over the course of 2 years, the team increased the coverage rate to over 90% and reduced the gap between the highest and lowest coverage schools from 78% to 23%. Although Amanda went on to focus on process redesign in other areas while coaching district teams across the country, she continued to think about substitute teaching. When Jill called almost a decade later asking about the potential to help HR teams think about the issue in a different way, Amanda knew it was possible to make the substitute teaching experience better.

Jill is a serial social entrepreneur: restless, optimistic, and almost always ready to throw herself at a new challenge. She's the founder of both Oakland's Museum of Children's Art (MOCHA) and Playworks, a 24-year-old national nonprofit focused on play and recess. Her introduction to substitute teaching came in the form of a number of different elementary school principals asking her if they could "borrow" their Playworks recess coach to fill in when they'd been unable to either attract or retain a sub for one of their classes. Jill always said no to this request, but it happened often enough, and in such a wide variety of school settings, that it sparked her curiosity.

Ultimately, this curiosity led Jill to a fellowship at Stanford's Hasso Plattner Institute of Design (better known as the d.school) where she had the opportunity to spend a year being immersed in the tools and mindsets of design. To say the very least, the year was a revelation. Jill had the chance to conduct hundreds of interviews with people connected to substitute teaching. She also tested trainings for subs, interviewed teachers and district administrators, engaged with high school students around their ideas for solutions, observed individuals going through the application process to become a sub, explored how temporary employees in the for-profit sector were treated as a point of comparison, and spent what could only be described as a luxurious amount of time making sense of all the information she was absorbing.

Beyond our own experiences, exploring the bigger world of substitute teaching has created lots of opportunities for us to become familiar with other people's experiments, and it turns out that there are quite a few "wins" out in the world.

"HACK"
n. a small, scrappy experiment that enables quick learning & requires very little expense or risk.

WE'RE QUICK!

We will introduce you to some of these in later chapters. You'll note that at times, their perspectives on the challenges of substitute teaching differ from ours. It's quite possible that your position on the hows and whys of substitute teaching may be different from ours as well. We're good with that. Our hope is that this book will inspire you to go on your own design journey—building empathy for the people affected by the substitute teaching experience, taking the time to define the problem within your context, and playing with the information you gather in a way that leads to some real-time prototyping. We've defined this book's (and our) success as: first, getting you, dear reader, to suspend your disbelief that it's possible to improve the state of substitute teaching; and second, getting you to try a hack—a small, scrappy experiment that enables quick learning and requires very little expense or risk. In our experience, this process leads to new perspectives, and innovative change.

What's Ahead

Design begins with empathy, and that's where we will start this book. We are going to tell you the story of a single day of substitute teaching through the lens of the different people connected to it. Whatever your role in the world of education, we want you to begin to build empathy for the people who rely on this system, from the substitutes themselves to the students, teachers, and the rest of the school team. We want to invite you to see the people who make up this system, to get curious about their experience, and to begin to think about how to make it better. That spark is what drives the design process.

Next, we'll step back to orient you to how substitute teaching works today, and hopefully illuminate what is often an invisible system. We've been surprised and humbled by what we didn't know, and want to share what we've learned. In the How Substitute Teaching Works Today chapter we'll lay out what the system looks like at both the school and district levels. This chapter also includes a few profiles of substitute teachers and quotes from teachers and students—to focus on the human side of this complex system.

Once we've taken a look at the bigger picture, we'll turn our attention to the reason we are here: making it work better. We'll begin with Start Where You Are, a chapter about improvement—working within the current system of your school or district. Drawing on our experience working side-by-side with school and district leaders, this chapter offers practical advice about what you can do today. As we will explain, we've boiled down sub strategy to one simple idea: getting subs to come back. We'll break down what we've learned about this—what you can do to encourage them to come back and work more in your school or district.

In the Design Lab chapter, we will invite you to begin to build a different future for substitute teaching. At Substantial we use a design-thinking approach to experiment with ideas to improve the substitute learning experience. At the heart of design work is the process of building empathy for the people you are designing with/for, and quickly trying out ideas in real settings. In this chapter we'll introduce you to the basics of design thinking and share some of what we've learned about using this approach. Design is best learned through doing, so we want to give you enough in this chapter to get started, but it's hard to convey the magic of design thinking in writing. You've got to try it to understand it—we hope that you emerge from the Design Lab chapter ready to begin learning by doing.

In the Opportunities chapter we will offer specific ideas for reimagining substitute teaching—ranging from minor shifts to more significant redesigns—with the hope that one of them inspires you to work on something similar in your own school or district. We've also included real-life examples and profiles of the innovators behind them.

Writing this book has been an extraordinary experience. It has provided an amazing opportunity for us to make meaning of our own work on substitute teaching, and given us access to inspiring people all across the country who were unwilling to settle for a dysfunctional status quo. Our hope, as you read the pages that follow, is that you will share in this experience. And our belief is that if you are willing to be open to imagining a new possibility and the idea that you—yes, you!—have the power to make a difference, we can collectively redesign the substitute teaching experience for everyone.

Time to get started!

Building Empathy: Parallel Journeys

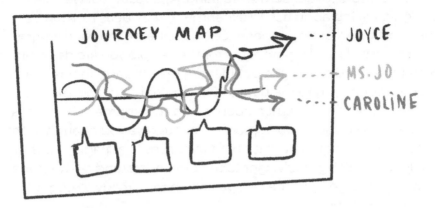

While we recognize that it's not exactly the usual way to start (and that the story that follows is actually a bit long), we'd like to invite you to come on a narrative journey with us: a day in the life of subbing. As you read each person's story, you'll be forming a visual map, a "journey map," of the process that they go through in order to accomplish their goal. In product design, engineers often use customer journey maps to better understand the experience of people who will use their solution.

A few things to keep in mind as you read this story:

1. We're hoping that this story will encourage you to recognize the power of empathy in understanding a system well enough to redesign it.
2. We want you to consider the importance of always asking "why?" And beyond the first "why," we find that asking "why" multiple times can lead to a much deeper understanding.
3. Storytelling is a fundamentally human capacity—we encourage you to tell stories about your own context as a way to win people over to your cause.

Here goes!

JOYCE

Let's begin with the sub herself. We'll get more into the statistics around subbing later in the book, but: a sub is more likely to be female. While requirements vary from state to state, a sub has most likely finished college, and while this journey mapping exercise is focused on just a single day, it's likely that in getting to this day, our substitute teacher—let's call her Joyce—has jumped through some significant hoops: studying for and then taking a test, being finger-printed, obtaining and submitting a TB test, being interviewed, and probably making two or three visits to the district office.

And again, while there are a myriad of ways in which Joyce may have gotten her assignment, for the purposes of this journey map let's imagine that she has signed up online to sub at a school where she has never been before. All Joyce really knows in advance is that it is a 3rd grade class at Magruder Elementary School, about a 25 min drive from her house.

The morning of the day that Joyce is subbing at Magruder, she wakes up early and packs a lunch; she has no way to know what the lunch situation is going to be. She arrives at the school about 25 min before she is supposed to start, and drives into the school parking lot to see if there is parking available. Finding none, she drives around the neighborhood for a bit, finally finding a space where it looks as though she'll be OK to leave the car for the entire school day.

Joyce makes her way to the school office where she finds a har-ried school secretary, Mrs. Carson, simultaneously juggling phones, attempting to calm an upset parent, and directing the copy machine repairman. Joyce waits a few minutes before introducing herself, and then asks where she should go and if the teacher has left a lesson plan. The response is disconcerting: Mrs. Carson looks at Joyce blankly before shuffling some papers on her desk and then holding up her hand in a gesture indicating that Joyce should wait. Joyce listens as

Mrs. Carson calls the principal's office—the door to the principal's office is actually open just a few feet away, and Joyce can almost hear what the principal is saying as the two discuss her situation. She tries not to be worried that no one seems to have been expecting her, or that it feels weird that these grownups who are only seated about 12 ft apart are talking on the phone. Ultimately the principal, Mr. Williams, comes out of his office, smiles, and introduces himself. He explains to Joyce that he will walk her to room 102, Ms. Jo's 3rd grade classroom, where he is sure Ms. Jo has left a lesson plan waiting.

It's worth noting here that while Joyce hasn't even met the students yet, her day has taken on a distinctly chaotic feeling. It's also worth noting that, in describing the situation at the school, our intent is not to characterize Mrs. Carson or Mr. Williams unkindly. Journey mapping their experiences is worth stepping away from Joyce's for a moment.

Mrs. Carson arrives at school every morning at a little after 7:00. She's usually either the first or second person on campus. Some-times the custodian has arrived before her and turned on all the lights, but just as often she's the first person on site. Most mornings begin fairly quietly. She makes coffee, listens to messages, and has 15–20 min to get organized. On some mornings there is something more unusual to deal with—like the time when she noticed the abandoned car someone had parked in the middle of the blacktop, or the more frequent issue of broken bottles and other detritus left behind by high school students who sometimes play basketball on the playground at night.

The phone messages are the more likely source of stress for Mrs. Carson—messages from families about student absences, and the more dreaded last-minute teacher absences. Mrs. Carson generally just skips over the ones from upset and irate parents, forwarding them to Mr. Williams' voicemail box. She also tries to get organized around the daily tasks she knows are going to need her attention. If there is a planned absence she's aware of, she looks in the teacher boxes to see if a lesson plan for the day has been left behind; teachers are supposed to leave them in the office, but many still leave them on their desks for the sub. Nothing about the process is particularly consistent, and it has never occurred to Mrs. Carson that she might have the authority to suggest they do things differently.

MR. WILLIAMS

(TIRED & BUSY)

Mr. Williams, meanwhile, has a 45 min commute each way to work, and this morning he's tired because he was at a school board meeting the night before. It was a contentious meeting that ran late, and he's feeling a bit grumpy. His day is looking complicated as he knows that he has a parent meeting first thing, and then needs to head immediately over to the district office for the elementary principals' meeting with the Chief Academic Officer to review the new standardized testing protocols. He also has a teacher on probation with whom he needs to sit down, and he's hoping that Operations will send over the copy machine repair guy, because their machine has been jamming paper and his teachers have been complaining bitterly.

Mr. Williams tries not to think about the substitute teacher situation at his school. Most of the teachers have a few consistent subs that they call on when they're absent, and Mrs. Carson is diligent about working the phones to get someone in the classroom when they need someone last minute. The situation is a lot better this year than last. Last year they ended up farming the students out to other classes about a third of the time, largely because Mrs. Rudy went out on maternity leave and they never managed to fill her long-term sub role. In any case, Mr. Williams has a lot of things to worry about and substitute teaching is nowhere near the top of his list.

Joyce, of course, knows none of this. She is appreciative that Mr. Williams walks her to the classroom, and sure enough, Ms. Jo has left a folder on her desk that says "sub plan." After Mr. Williams leaves, she looks inside and finds the day's schedule and the attendance sheet with a few notes written in the margins about individual students—nothing damning, but not particularly helpful—things like "may need to take a break" or "will be happy to help." There is a stack of worksheets with a post-it on it that says "for group time," and a separate sheet that has some hard-to-follow instructions around Writer's Workshop and a Mrs. Donahue coming to help during math.

Joyce realizes that the students are starting to arrive, so she goes and stands by the door to welcome each of them individually, introduce herself, and ask the students their names. She had been taught to do this the very first time she ever subbed; the office manager at the school had advised her that this was a way to get the students to tell you their actual names before they had a chance to organize into a rebellious force against you. At the time, Joyce had thought the office manager's tone was a little worrisome and that the advice seemed paranoid, but she has nonetheless been doing it ever since, and has found that it helps her make a human connection with at least some of the kids to start the day.

Ms. Jo, meanwhile, is home and sick as a dog with strep throat. She had known she was getting sick, but had been putting it off

because her usual sub, a former teacher named Mr. McManus who took early retirement, is traveling in Scotland with his wife and their daughter. The thought of leaving her class to a complete stranger makes Ms. Jo a bit crazy, and while she had spent a couple of hours pulling together some materials for the day, and even driving over to the district office to make copies of the worksheets, the whole exercise felt futile and frustrating to her. Ms. Jo was convinced that the sub would never use the materials she left behind, and leaving instructions for a complete stranger is an almost impossible task.

Mostly, Ms. Jo is worried about her students—two in particular. Caroline has been making steady progress around taking risks and participating actively in class, and a bad experience with a sub could set her way back. And Ms. Jo can almost count on the fact that Teddy is going to act out. He is high energy and prone to engaging in attention-getting behaviors, falling back on negative attention when that is what works. Having a sub also means a lot of extra work for Ms. Jo when she comes back from being sick.

Caroline has been looking forward to class today. She is excited for Writer's Workshop because she and Ms. Jo have been talking through a story idea that she's keen to work on, and Ms. Jo has promised that today Caroline can choose the game they all play together at recess. Caroline has decided that she's going to choose Gaga Ball, partly because she knows it's Teddy's favorite, and she hopes he'll appreciate her having noticed.

Two other quick perspectives, and then back to Joyce. Mariam was working in the Payroll department when the job of sub coordinator became available. It was technically a promotion and she was ready for a new challenge, so she applied.

MARIAM

At first she had tried to learn more about the systems in place and figure out how to make them work better, but quickly the sheer volume of demands made it impossible to do anything other than respond to whatever disaster floated highest on the HR director's list.

Mariam had met Joyce twice—once when she came in for her interview and a second time when she came in for the mandatory 4-hr onboarding orientation. She had seemed nice, and Mariam recalled that she had mentioned being interested in becoming a full-time teacher. Joyce had not received any negative reports through the system and so Mariam had not had an opportunity to think about her since the onboarding.

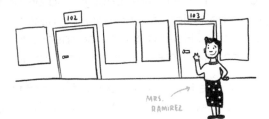

MRS. RAMIREZ

And finally, Mrs. Ramirez is the 2nd grade teacher in the classroom next to Ms. Jo. She's known Ms. Jo for a long time and has offered to check in while Ms. Jo is out. (Ms. Jo does the same for her.) Mrs. Ramirez doesn't really admit it to herself, but knowing that Ms. Jo is going to be out fills her with a mild sense of dread. She's not looking forward to meeting the new sub, she worries for Ms. Jo's students, and, frankly, being in a classroom next to one where a sub is present can be very disruptive. Mrs. Ramirez feels a bit guilty, but decides to put off going to say hello to the sub until they're scheduled to go out for morning recess.

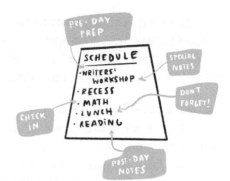

Back in Joyce's classroom, things are going better than you might expect. The class has some well-established routines and there are a couple of students who are excited to step up and explain how things are done. "Group time" turns out to be a morning check-in, with everyone seated on the rug. There are a couple of boys who want to talk about the local baseball team, and Joyce wins some quick and easy points by knowing the names of some of the players. When they transition to their seats at group tables to begin the worksheets, some diligently focus on the assignment, but a significant number stare into space or begin whispering. Joyce is moving among the different tables, helping as needed. One table has completely abandoned the worksheet, and she sends them each to find a book they want to look at on their own.

Writer's Workshop is a little bumpier. Joyce isn't entirely clear on what they're supposed to be working on, and neither are the students. Caroline remains seated at her table even after everyone else has gotten up to go to the writing station. When Joyce asks if there is anything she can do to help, Caroline just shakes her head "no" and lets out a little sniffle, momentarily making Joyce feel terrible.

It is finally 10:40 and time for recess. Mrs. Ramirez sticks her head into Ms. Jo's class and is visibly relieved to see that there is a modicum of order. The children call out "Good morning, Mrs. Ramirez!" and begin putting their things away in preparation for going outside. Joyce introduces herself to Mrs. Ramirez and feels a wave of relief wash over her. She's a third of the way through the day.

Out at recess, Joyce feels her sense of relief deepen a bit. Mrs. Ramirez is friendly, albeit a little distant. In any case, Joyce is just happy to have another grownup around for the moment. The kids seem happy. All, at least, except for Caroline, whom Joyce assumes is still upset about whatever it was that was bothering her during Writer's Workshop. The time flies by, as does the time before lunch when they return to the classroom. Mrs. Donahue comes in to take a group of students to work on math. Elise, one of the students who stays behind, explains in a theatrical whisper that Mrs. Donahue works with the "*emerging* math learners." The students who do stay in the class seem to know what to do, and begin to take out their math workbooks and some other materials. This gives Joyce a moment to review Ms. Jo's notes in anticipation of the afternoon.

A bell announces lunchtime, and once again Mrs. Ramirez pokes her head in. "We can all walk to the cafeteria together," she offers. Joyce is hoping she doesn't seem pathetically grateful. The students walk quietly in the hallway, but the din in the cafeteria is almost deafening. Mrs. Ramirez speaks loudly to be heard over all the noise, "You don't have to stay here the whole time, but you need to be back by 12:30 to walk the students from recess to class." And with that, she turns and leaves.

Joyce looks around the cafeteria and sees a few cafeteria workers, a woman she recognizes from the office, and Mr. Williams. He gives a friendly wave and resumes his conversation with a group of students. Joyce hesitates briefly, but then decides it's probably best if she goes back to the classroom to have lunch and a bit of a break before the afternoon.

Substantial Classrooms: Redesigning the Substitute Teaching Experience

When she meets up with the students at the end of lunch recess, Joyce has a sinking feeling that the afternoon is going to be more challenging. While the other classes are all lining up, Ms. Jo's class is still a bit scattered and Tommy is nowhere to be found. Mr. Williams comes over to ask if Joyce needs help, which ends up making her feel even more flustered. Tommy appears out of nowhere and Joyce manages to corral Ms. Jo's class back into the school.

The afternoon involves some choice time and free reading. And while things start out fine, Joyce is increasingly aware that not only is Tommy not engaged in any of the options, he's actively distracting the other students. Her efforts to engage him divert him a bit, but the other students are clearly watching closely to see how she will react. By 1:45, Joyce is pretty much out of tricks. Some of the students are creating illustrations to go with their Writer's Workshop projects, and when Joyce suggests that Tommy might want to draw something to go along with his, he announces in a very loud voice, "This is stupid!"

The very loud voice in Joyce's head says a number of different things, mostly along the lines of, "You can't talk to me that way!" Something about the way the other students audibly gasp is a clue to Joyce that this is not the moment to stand and deliver. Tommy is looking theatrically defiant, until Joyce laughs and says, "You know, I agree. Should we go out for an afternoon recess?"

In an instant, Tommy's stance shifts from defiant to outraged. "You can't do that!" he insists. "In point of fact," Joyce counters, "I can, and I am. Who wants to lead a game?"

The students are stunned—none more so than Caroline, who surprises herself by raising her hand and volunteering, "I can run Gaga Ball." The other students stand and prepare to go outside in the same manner they had earlier. Joyce waves through the window of Mrs. Ramirez's class as the students head out for their bonus recess.

The rest of the day goes pretty well. They sit on the rug and share stories about their favorite recess games and the games they would invent if they were game inventors. Joyce reads a couple of books aloud and, mercifully, the final bell rings.

After the students have all gone, Joyce straightens up the classroom a bit and leaves a note for Ms. Jo thanking her and telling her that her students were very cooperative and helpful. She stops by the office to say goodbye, but Mrs. Carson is on the phone and Mr. Williams is not in his office. Joyce waits briefly, wondering if there is something she should do, but decides it's OK to leave when Mrs. Carson gives her a friendly, dismissive wave. Ultimately, Joyce decides it was a good day when she returns to her car and there is no ticket on the windshield.

One Day, Many Experiences

Whoa. That's exhausting, right? And we mostly focused on Joyce's journey—each of the people we mentioned had a full set of experiences during that day, all intersecting and influencing one another. It's a lot to navigate, but it's also really clear that being aware of these parallel journeys has profound implications for how one goes about trying to solve—and even define—"the problem."

We offer this story to demonstrate the surprisingly significant reach and influence of a day of subbing, but also to emphasize what we consider the "magic shortcut" of design: empathy. We have consistently found that digging deeply into individual stories unearths surprising universal truths about the system's dynamics. For a human used to taking a more analytical approach, this can almost feel like cheating. But when combined with rapid testing, it allows you to quickly recognize which ideas are more fringe, and which actually generate resonance among the people who will use your solution. Like most mature systems (and by mature, we mean old, entrenched, and crazy-making), substitute teaching can feel like an intractable problem, generating a level of resignation and hopelessness that compounds institutional resistance to change. Design thinking, though, enters into it all with small, quirky hacks, and just enough sizzle and sex appeal to be disarming. It also offers a degree of freedom: you are not trying to design for the entirety of the challenge, but in following the inspiration that a few individuals offer, you can find a point of entry into the work that feels both hopeful and doable.

That being said, it does help to have some understanding of the larger system you are hoping to influence, so let's dive into the current state of subbing.

EMPATHY!

DESIGN THINKING

HOW SUBSTITUTE TEACHING WORKS TODAY

ACADEMICY CHAPTER

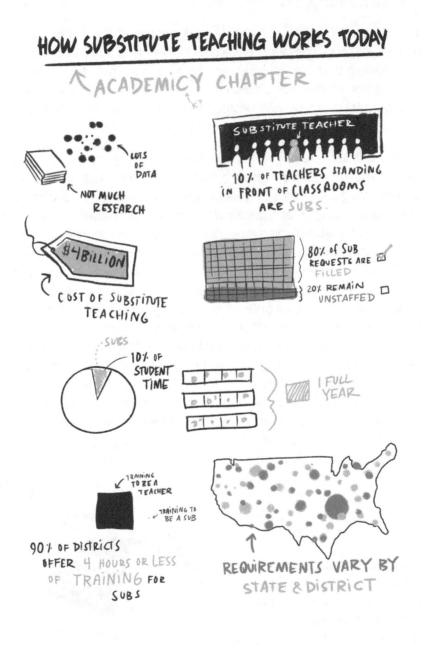

LOTS OF DATA

NOT MUCH RESEARCH

SUBSTITUTE TEACHER

10% OF TEACHERS STANDING IN FRONT OF CLASSROOMS ARE SUBS.

$4 BILLION

COST OF SUBSTITUTE TEACHING

80% OF SUB REQUESTS ARE FILLED

20% REMAIN UNSTAFFED

SUBS

10% OF STUDENT TIME

I FULL YEAR

TRAINING TO BE A TEACHER

TRAINING TO BE A SUB

90% OF DISTRICTS OFFER 4 HOURS OR LESS OF TRAINING FOR SUBS

REQUIREMENTS VARY BY STATE & DISTRICT

How Substitute Teaching Works Today

This chapter requires some caveats. First: we are not academics. Nerdy, yes. Formal researchers, not so much. Our point of view on addressing the substitute teaching experience is that, in general, the best place to begin is by conducting empathy interviews in your own school or district, and getting your arms around the strengths and challenges of the system you currently have. That being said, it's also useful to have a bigger picture understanding of the state of subbing. Along our own journey, we've been surprised—and even caught off guard—by the issues that have come up. We are hoping that this section might serve to prepare you a bit for this. It's probably best to think of this section less as an exhaustive review, and more the *What to Expect When You're Expecting* for anyone interested in tackling the substitute teaching issue.

If you are an academic (or friendly with one) we hope this chapter also starts your wheels turning. This is an area primed for research. Almost every school district uses an online system for tracking sub requests and assignments, which creates a rich data set. There is also an enticing research possibility at the state level because the same credentialing agencies issue sub permits and teaching certifications.

There really isn't a lot of research on the state of substitute teaching. For those of you who want to dig a little deeper, we've included the small list we *have* found in the Resources section at the end of the book. In this next chapter, we will draw on these resources, plus the hundreds of interviews we've conducted over the past 3 years as part of our effort to paint a clear picture of how substitute teaching works today. To help us keep sight of the humanity of the people involved in this larger system, we've included individual profiles and quotes. So, here goes . . .

Surprising Stats

There are a few key statistics we frequently use to spark peoples' interest in the issue of subbing:

- At any given moment, **10%** of the teachers standing in front of US classrooms are subs. This means the average student in the US will have **one full year** of their K-12 education taught by a substitute teacher.[1]
- 90% of districts offer 4 hrs or less of training for subs.[2]
- Of the 50 states, only 15 require that a sub has a BA, and five of the states don't even require high school completion (though many of these "requirements" have loopholes that we will discuss more later).[3]
- The average sub coverage rate across the country is 80%—meaning that for every 100 subs requested, 80 subs are actually placed in classrooms.[4]
- As a nation, we spend $4 billion dollars annually on substitute teachers.[5]

---

1   SubNation, Gatehouse Media (https://gatehousenews.com/subnation).
2   Substitute Teaching Division of STEDI (http://stedi.org).
3   Status of Substitute Teachers: A State-By-State Summary, National Education Association (and our own research and analysis).
4   Frontline Institute National Teacher Absence and Substitute Data Report (http://frontlineinstitute.com).
5   Teacher Absence as a Leading Indicator of Student Achievement, Raegan Miller, National Council on Teacher Quality (NCTQ).

How does it feel to leave your class with a substitute teacher?

"IT'S STRESSFUL to try to explain to SOMEONE IN WRITING how to do YOUR job."

"I get ANXIETY about how the class will behave."

"NERVE-WRACKING"

MOST COMMON ANSWER

"IF THE SUB IS SOMEONE I'M FAMILIAR WITH, I'M much more comfortable"

RETIRED TEACHER

WORKING ARTIST

Who Are Substitute Teachers?

One of the most exciting—and complicating—elements of substitute teaching is the unbelievable variety of people who serve as substitutes. They come from many different backgrounds and are in every phase of professional life. Some are teachers, subbing in retirement after a full career. Others have worked with kids in after-school or summer camp settings. Still others are new to working with students and have no background or training in education. Some have subbed for years, but many are in their first few assignments. We've included a few profiles in this chapter, but they couldn't possibly capture the range.

The makeup of sub pools varies dramatically by district, even within the same state or region. In one school district we work with, there are many retired teachers serving as subs, and just 28% of their subs are under 50 years old. In another district, the majority of their subs are in their late 30s and early 40s and work at just one or two schools a few times a month; we have a hunch that these are mostly parents.

The substitute teaching population, as a subset of the larger teaching force, is disproportionately female and white,[6] though you will meet some innovators later in the book who are exploring substitute teaching as an opportunity to diversify the pipeline of new teachers.

---

6   National Center for Education Statistics, School and Staffing Survey, 2011–2012.

Requirements to be a Sub

There are significant variations across the states around the require-ments for being a sub. At the time of writing, 1 state requires that you have the same credentials as a teacher, 15 states require a college degree, and 5 states don't even require a high school degree.[7] All states seem to feel strongly that you can't have com-mitted a felony, nor can you test positive for TB. Many of the states require that you take a test to be eligible, and a few require basic training (think an online course or 1-day workshop) to qualify for the necessary permit. And while many states rely heavily on retired teachers to be subs, some states have eligibility restrictions on how soon a teacher can sub after retiring and/or if a retired teacher can sub while receiving retirement benefits.

Digging a little deeper, one discovers that there are loopholes for some of these sub requirements. In California, for example, while a BA is nominally required, there is an exemption available for current college students with 90 credits.[8] Many exemptions and loopholes are framed as eligibility for "emergency" or temporary credentials, though the state of emergency has now been ongoing for decades in most places, and might be more accurately defined as the status quo.

---

7   Ibid.
8   Emergency Substitute Teaching Permit for Prospective Teachers, California Commission on Teacher Credentialing (http://ctc.ca.gov).

Carol Zink

Carol Zink began her career in the Navy where she served during the Cold War, intensifying her interest in Russia and Russian history. After the Navy, Carol worked in the software industry for many years, and then decided that teaching would be a more fulfilling use of her time. She became a teacher at the independent Harker School, where she taught AP European history and modern world history for 11 years before retiring from full-time teaching.

But Carol's second retirement didn't last too long before she became a sub at some local public schools. "People go into subbing because they miss teaching," she explained. "It isn't about the income—I love teaching."

Nonetheless, Carol initially found substitute teaching to be a surprisingly isolating experience. Teachers were friendly in a surface way, she explains. "They'd say 'ask me if you need any help' but I knew they didn't mean it. Teachers don't have time to talk, especially if you are just there for a day." There was no interaction with any of the other subs; the days simply weren't structured in a way where that was feasible. In stark contrast with her experience of being a teacher, Carol was surprised to find that the only adult interaction the experience of subbing afforded was with the administrative staff in the office, and even that was very limited.

While teaching in the classroom, Carol had been able to develop significant relationships with her students. These were at the core of her ability to be effective as an educator. Carol had known that trust was essential to working well with adolescents, and the substitute teaching experience made that even more apparent. "I don't like being a cop. It's so much better when you know the students." She was acutely aware that the trust went both ways; she needed the students to feel like they knew her as well. "Kids want to know that it won't be a wasted day for them—you have to establish that quickly."

While Carol acknowledges that the transition was not without challenges, she is also quick to point out that subbing has some distinct advantages as well. From embracing the flexibility so that she can do more traveling, to weaving her varied life experiences into the classroom, Carol finds substitute teaching to be an excellent fit for her current stage of life. And as a bonus, Carol adds, she loves that she doesn't have to "worry about things like meetings—no one likes meetings . . . ." Now she mainly subs at Harker, and enjoys interacting with her former colleagues as well as the younger siblings of students she taught. Because the teachers at Harker know her, they trust her to actually teach rather than just "babysit" students. Carol finds this much more enjoyable.

A Transitional Role

One of the defining characteristics of the substitute teaching system is the constant churn as subs transition to other jobs and new subs enter the system. As one of the original gig economy jobs (where workers are paid per task or project), substitute teaching has also been an in-between job, easy for people to turn to during moments of transition.

Substitute teaching has long been a pathway into the profession for newly credentialed teachers searching for a first job. In recent years, the teacher shortage has meant that an increasing number of new teachers are hired directly out of school programs where they are studying to become teachers; they never formally enter the job pool. Anecdotally, we know many people try out substitute teaching, have a traumatic early experience, and decide it's not for them. Many of these people are curious about teaching and are using substitute teaching as a way to try on the role and see if they want to become teachers. And while any teacher will tell you that being a substitute is very different than being a permanent classroom teacher, there usually isn't anyone helping subs to see the distinctions, or to make meaning of their early experiences.

The Need for Subs

Substitute teaching is how the education sector has decided to handle an inevitable situation: teachers will need to be absent from the classroom. Sometimes it's because they are sick—they do, after all, work with lots of children who carry lots of germs—and sometimes it's because they are engaged in things related to their jobs, like professional development or special duties.

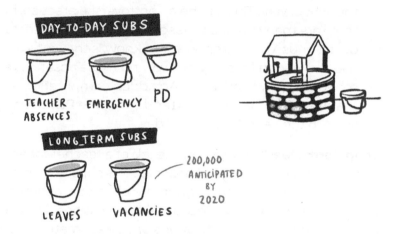

There are several different reasons why substitute teachers are needed. It's helpful to think of them in five buckets:

1. **Day-to-Day Needs:** Filling in for a teacher for a few days.

    a. **Teacher Absences:** Think of all the reasons you might miss work—you are sick, your kid is sick, you have a medical appointment, you're traveling to your niece's wedding, you need a mental health day, etc. Teachers are no different, and they need subs to fill in for them. Most day-to-day absences are known ahead, so teachers usually prepare lesson plans.

b. **Emergency Absences:** (A special category of day-to-day absences.) When a teacher is unexpectedly absent— think a sudden stomach bug or family emergency. When we've run the numbers, about 20% of sub requests are submitted at 5:00 the night before the absence, or later. Most schools require that teachers keep "emergency plans" for just these instances.

c. **Professional Development:** School districts often schedule professional development for teachers during the school year. This can be a controversial practice, but there are many practical reasons schools and districts do it. For us, what's important to know is that subs are usually needed for a day or two, and these absences are scheduled way in advance. An added complication is that many teachers often attend the same PD, creating a spike in the need for subs in 1 day.

2. **Long-Term Needs:** Assuming the job of a teacher for an extended period of time. In most systems subs in long-term positions receive a slightly higher rate of pay. Sometimes they are required to have additional certifications, but usually not the same level of certifications or subject matter exper- tise as a permanent classroom teacher.

a. **Leaves:** When there is a permanent teacher in the class, but they need to be absent for an extended period of time. Usually they are on maternity/paternity leave, or they or a loved one have a major health issue. Usually (but not always) the class will have established rou- tines, but the substitute teacher will still need to do some planning.

b. **Vacancies:** (A special category of long-term assign- ments.) When there is no permanent teacher, either because one could not be hired before the school year or someone has quit unexpectedly during the school year.

In this case there isn't much of a foundation for the substitute teacher to work with, and usually no one else is doing the lesson planning.[9]

In the last few years, the issue of teacher absence has received a lot of attention. It's a complicated issue, but the general trend is that there has been an increase in teacher absence. We've included some research on the issue of teacher absence in the Resources chapter, but in the spirit of full transparency we should acknowledge that we lean toward the belief that focusing on teacher absence is often a red herring, distracting the conversation away from the more relevant issue of teaching conditions. This can lead people to the (we think false) conclusion that teachers are to blame.

The last point we want to make about teacher absence as it relates to substitutes is that the two are weirdly interdependent. One of the surprising things we've seen is that many teachers really don't want to have a sub in the classroom because they fear it will be disruptive. And because subs are hard to find, schools often have a hard time scheduling professional development days. One particularly painful result of the sub system not working well is that it exacerbates the challenges of working in a school: being disincentivized from taking a sick day when you're sick, and not being able to get the professional development that you need. These conditions lead to greater turnover among teachers, which leads to higher demand for substitute teachers, and greater stress on an already challenged system. Vicious cycle defined!

9   Sutcher, L., Darling-Hammond, L., & Carver-Thomas, D. (2016). *A coming crisis in teaching? Teacher supply, demand, and shortages in the U.S.*. Palo Alto, CA: Learning Policy Institute.

Todd Berman

Todd Berman's innovation was a bit more personal—more like a hack that he transformed into a lifestyle. Todd is a visual artist, and after a year as an AmeriCorps member at a nonprofit helping high school students transition from school to careers, he wanted sustainable employment that would still allow him enough time to make his art. He tried temping, but wasn't wild about the experience. Several teachers who saw how much he enjoyed working with high school students suggested that he try subbing. Todd took the CBEST, got his TB test and fingerprints, and signed up.

"I remember there was a half day training," Todd says about his subbing beginnings, now well over a decade ago. "They spent almost all the time explaining to us how the assignment and payroll systems worked, and then there was about 30 min of Q&A with a current sub, and that was it."

Todd describes being surprised by the lack of structure and consistency for subs. Each classroom was different, and no one was available to answer his questions. He started out by subbing at the school where he'd worked as an AmeriCorps member, and that made things a bit easier, but he also wanted to explore other schools and different age groups. He ultimately decided that high schools were his subbing sweet spot.

His big subbing breakthrough—the initial hack—came about because Todd is never without his sketchbook. During an early subbing experience, he pulled it out to sketch while the students were working on an assignment, and they asked him about it. Sharing his art with them turned out to be an opportunity to build connection and respect. In another classroom, students were given an assignment to interview him and record the interviews. He added an art element, and this memorable, student-led experience became his marker of what was possible when the grownups involved remembered that it was the students' classroom as much as anyone's.

Todd built relationships around his art, and subbing started to feel less hectic. He would sub only for pre-arranged absences, and school secretaries squirreled away materials for his art projects with the students. He collaborated with the teachers, identifying arts activities related to what the students were studying. He became involved with the Alameda County Office of Education's Integrated Learning Specialists Program which, as Todd puts it, "opened up a world of approaches and opportunities to deepen my practice." Now an instructor with the program, Todd works with the San Francisco Arts Commission, exploring graffiti art with students, and heads up the Arts Education Alliance of the Bay Area. He is convinced that the experiences have shaped him as an artist interested in making collaborative art. They helped him develop his ability to get people involved, and to make learning visible.

Substitute Teaching as a System

To understand how substitute teaching works today, it's helpful to think about it as a system. Like all established systems, it is self-reinforcing and nearly invisible to those who interact with it. But if we are going to address the challenges, we need to understand how the formal structures and informal dynamics come together to create the (largely stable) system that we see today. Sally Osberg and Roger Martin write about precisely this in their book, *Getting Beyond Better*, where they define *equilibrium* as a balanced, stable system that tends to persist in its current state even when it is unproductive, unless there is intentional action to shift it. We like to think about substitute teaching as being in a state of *unproductive equilibrium*.

Historical news articles and glancing mentions in research about how school districts developed indicate that substitute teaching as we know it emerged around the same time as school districts. During the administrative progressive era—roughly the 1890s to 1920s, when reforms sought to improve government efficiencies through nonpolitical "technocrats"—school districts were created to bring scale and efficiency to back-office services.[10] Within this effort, a new system emerged to help schools manage contingency staffing when teachers were out of the classroom. Prior to that era, most schools had a few individual subs, but there was no larger system. One innovative attempt to address this was the creation of

10   Boyd, W., Kerchner, C., & Blyth, M. (Eds.). (2008). *The transformation of great American School Districts: How big cities are reshaping public education.* Cambridge, MA: Harvard Education Press.

centralized pools of substitute teachers who could be dispatched to various schools in the same geographic area.

The basic system has been relatively stable for the last 100 years. Here's how it works.

A school district will hire a centralized pool of substitute teachers who can work at any school within the district. From what we can tell, the basic profile of a substitute teacher hasn't changed dramatically. It's always been a temporary, at-will position—that's why we think of subs as the original gig workers.

Teachers report when they are going to be absent, and then subs choose which assignments they will accept from the list of requests. While it used to be the job of central dispatchers, the requests and assignments are now managed on an online platform called a sub assignment system. Teachers log in and report their absence. Substitutes log in, peruse the list, and choose the jobs they want.

There is also an informal system for assigning subs to jobs. Most schools have a "shortlist" of substitute teachers they like working with, and many teachers have relationships with favorite subs. They call those subs first, and then put the job into the system as "prearranged." In general, the informal system works better than the formal system, and schools that have strong relationships with subs have better coverage.

In most districts there is a sub coordinator who is responsible for the day-to-day operation of the sub system. This person usually has a clerical or technical background and is a master at multitasking. Watching them in the morning is something like watching a 911 operator: they are calm and focused as they field urgent calls from schools while making personal calls to ask subs to take specific jobs. Typically, they are the first person in the building in the morning and will have a few hours of intense focus before shifting to processing new-hire paperwork. They also investigate issues that come up, from subs who act inappropriately with students to incidents when subs are mistreated. In larger systems, a small team of two or three people often share these duties.

Substitute teachers are hired at volume, with minimal interview or selection process time. Once hired, they typically receive an orientation that includes basic tips for classroom management and directions on how to use the assignment system. This initial training typically lasts 4 hrs or less, and is often the last time the substitute teacher will receive training.

In virtually every district we've looked at, pay for substitute teachers is exceptionally low—often in the same range as retail and fast food jobs. In most places, substitute teachers do not receive benefits and are paid only for the days they work. This is a huge and defining issue for substitute teaching, and we strongly believe subs should be paid more.

How Much, Exactly, Do Subs Make?

Sub pay is determined by a number of different factors. Generally speaking, long-term sub jobs pay more than short-term jobs, and subs who have more education and/or a teaching license get paid more than those without. In some states, subs who have taken the http://STEDI.org (Utah State's Substitute Teaching Institute) training are also eligible for a higher pay rate. The biggest determinant of sub pay is regional, with pay rates being determined at the district level. As of this writing, we've seen day rates as low as $60 and as high as $250, with rates occasionally being increased during teacher strikes.

What's it like to have a sub?

Outsourcing

There has been one major innovation in substitute teaching systems in the last few decades: outsourcing. Many school systems now outsource substitute teaching to specialized temp firms. This industry has grown significantly over the last two decades. For example, Kelly Education Services now employs over 64,000 substitute teachers and provides substitute staffing to 7000+ schools across the country.[11] Our observation is that outsourcing simply replaces the administrative functions HR was previously doing. In general, it appears that outsource firms focus more on recruitment and are thus often able to provide better coverage.

Outsourcing itself has been the target of some disruption in recent years as start-ups have entered the field, many of which are endeavoring to improve the technology behind the recruitment and placement of subs. We profile Sarah Cherry Rice of Parachute Education later in the book; Parachute initially started down this route but has since pivoted in their approach. Another company we've worked with is Swing Education, founded by former K-12 administrator Mike Teng, who knew first hand the frustration of not having the subs that were needed. Mike and team initially focused on automating and coordinating the texting and assigning of subs, but ultimately shifted to recruitment when their absence of sales compelled them to ask themselves the basic business question: "How are you going to help schools in the way that they want to be helped?"

---

11   Kelly Educational Staffing, kellyeducationalstaffing.us.

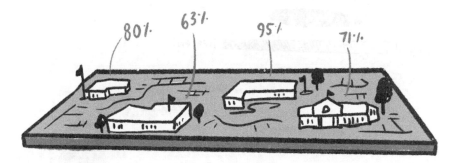

The Impact of Uneven Coverage

In the vast majority of places, substitute teachers choose when and where they work. This level of autonomy, flexibility, and control is one of the things that makes substitute teaching attractive as a job, but it also often results in uneven coverage at different schools within a school district. Some schools have plenty of substitute teachers and virtually every sub job is covered. Other schools struggle to attract and retain substitute teachers for a variety of reasons, so they have more unfilled substitute jobs. As elementary principal Megan Burnham explains, "It's hard when my teachers aren't at school and we don't have a sub. Honestly, it's one of the most stressful things in my life."

Chicago Public Schools provides a vivid example of this. According to a recent NPR analysis of substitute coverage data, the Chicago schools that serve a majority of black and Latinx students have a 65% coverage rate—almost one-third of the time a sub is needed, no one shows up. In fact, 62 of the district's 520 schools have less than half of their requests filled. By contrast, at majority white or racially mixed schools, 80% of sub requests were filled.[12]

---

12   WBEZ Chicago NPR, Sarah Karp, "1 In 3 Chicago Public Schools Went Without A Teacher For a Year."

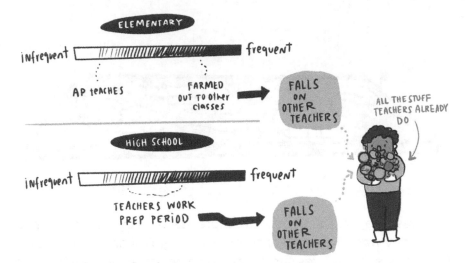

Since substitute teachers can accept jobs at any time, schools don't know if they will have an unstaffed classroom until just before school begins. This creates a stressful and sometimes chaotic situation as the staff figure out a Plan B. If this happens infrequently, schools will often have an assistant principal, teacher, coach, or special teacher (like the art or science teacher) cover the classroom. This pulls them away from their typical duties, which causes disruption, but isn't a big deal if it doesn't happen all the time.

Elementary schools that have high teacher absences will typically "farm out" an unstaffed class. Principal Burnham describes the process: "Say it's a 5th grade class with no sub. We will break the class up and send them to other classes, so three or four go to a 1st grade class, a few more to a 3rd grade class and so on. It disrupts the entire school." Though students from the unstaffed class will usually bring a packet of worksheets or other independent work to do at the back of the room, normal instruction has not only been disrupted for them, but also for the classroom that takes on these additional students.

At the secondary level, teachers often will sub for each other during their prep periods. An unstaffed class might have six different teachers throughout the day, each subbing during what would normally be their prep period. Teachers usually receive extra pay for either having extra students or working during their prep period. Sometimes this extra pay is appreciated, but if it's happening too frequently principals (rightfully) worry about teacher burnout.

A common strategy for addressing this challenge is to assign substitute teachers to work full time at schools that struggle to get enough sub coverage. There are a variety of ways districts structure the role, but the basic idea is that a sub reports to the same school every morning, and the school assigns them to cover whichever absence they think has the highest need. This gives principals more flexibility, and in our interviews we found that substitute teachers like these roles because they feel they are part of the school team. These subs are usually paid the long-term sub rate, but it's difficult for districts to keep these subs covering day-to-day absences because they are often slotted into long-term assignments.

What Happens in the Classroom

While we need to understand the larger system, our main focus is on what happens in the classroom. By far the most common theme we hear in our conversations about what happens in the classroom is some version of "subs need better classroom management skills." We've spent a fair amount of time thinking about how we might meet this need, and experimenting with professional development for subs. What we have learned is that the literature around classroom management techniques for teachers is focused on consistency and routines. Big picture: the advice for classroom management just doesn't translate into the world of substitute teaching.

Here's how it works at the classroom level today: teachers are responsible for creating a plan for a day on which they will be absent. It's usually called a "sub plan," and is some combination of a lesson plan, a description of how things work in the classroom, and tips—like which students are best to ask for help. There is no standard format for this, so each teacher creates their own. Not surprisingly, the formats and quality of the written directions vary greatly. Substitutes must find, read, and interpret these plans quickly. As you'll read in the next chapter, we've gone deep on this part of the challenge and created an online tool to make it easier for schools to prepare for and welcome subs.

Each class has their own rules and routines and, occasionally, their own set of expectations for how students behave with subs. Again, subs must quickly figure out these rules and establish their own authority within the room. As you might recall from your own time with subs, students often challenge subs. While this is partially about students testing boundaries, it's also a manifestation of our cultural narratives around substitute teachers. From *Miss Nelson Is Missing* (spoiler alert: children's book in which an exasperated teacher disguises herself as a mean sub so her students will come to appreciate her) to Key and Peele's *Substitute Teacher* sketches (worth Googling if you haven't seen them), subs are usually portrayed as mean or incompetent. These narratives seep into how students behave, how families talk about subs, and how teachers treat their temporary colleagues.

Special Education

Special education programs rely on subs for both special education teachers and special education paraprofessionals—often referred to as "paras." The shortages for these roles are off the charts. This area hasn't been one where we have actively engaged yet, but the stories we have gathered—of special education teachers being compelled to find their own subs, of paras running classes, of people with no training being assigned to special education classes—have made it abundantly clear that the issue around substitute teaching and special education is nothing short of a civil rights issue.

Why Isn't Substitute Teaching Receiving More Attention?

It can be perplexing to parents and other external partners that there is not more work happening around substitute teaching. Once you see the substitute teaching challenge for what it is, it's hard to unsee it. But it remains the "elephant in the classroom." We want to help illuminate some of the dynamics at play so you can better understand why this is, and we invite you to consider the facts with an orientation toward empathy for the people responsible for making this 100-year-old system run smoothly within your community.

We've synthesized it into four defining characteristics of substitute teaching that conspire to reinforce the status quo. From a design perspective, we sometimes try to think of these four aspects as design constraints: the defining realities that guide our choices in developing solutions. While constraints can sound limiting, there are all sorts of examples of how constraints actually promote creativity— from the structure of a haiku to the rules of basketball.

Justin Davis

Justin Davis spent 2 years as a fellow in the Central Falls' Warrior Teaching Fellows program before deciding to leave teaching to attend divinity school. Justin had known since high school that he was interested in youth development, and while attending Rhode Island College, his path began to move in that direction. He worked in special education and paid his way through school as a campus resident advisor. After college, he found a job at a group home, and from there made the jump to the Central Falls fellowship. He was placed at the Central Falls Middle School for both of his 2 years.

During his time there, the Central Falls district had six fellows, enabling the principal to divide up the subbing responsibilities according to each fellow's skills and strengths. Being a fellow, Justin says, "was both awesome and absurdly challenging." He had the opportunity to become an integral part of the community in a role he said was like being "a Swiss Army knife"—doing whatever was needed when it came to working directly with students. Each day was different, requiring him to start the day fresh. He had no idea what he'd be doing if he wasn't in a longer term sub assignment. He was a part of three separate long-term assignments during his tenure, including 4 months covering daily for two science classes. Justin describes the relationships that developed as a result of his consistent placement at the middle school as the key to his success in subbing.

In his first year, the fellows were allowed to shadow the teachers with whom they'd be working that year, allowing them to come to know the students and their routines. While this was helpful, he is quick to point out two specific relationships that emerged organically from the shadowing experience. The two teachers Justin shadowed became his mentors, and he would turn to them frequently, seeking advice, feedback, and support when things were challenging. Beyond the informal support, Central Falls also introduced induction specialists during his second year of service. While the induction specialists focused primarily on new teachers, they were also available to observe the teaching fellows and provide feedback. "We weren't left completely alone."

Like everyone we talked to about the Central Falls Teaching Fellowship, Justin mentioned the importance of the program's founder and leader, Jay Midwood (also profiled later in the opportunities chapter). "You need some kind of Jay," Justin observed laughingly. "Jay is encouraging but realistic; he's direct and accountable. Jay has a vision, and he won't settle for someone just covering the class. You don't need all this in one person, but you need it to be present, and you need them to prioritize other people being equipped to succeed."

Justin decided to move on during his second year. He realized that he had given all he could, and he recognized the very real danger of burnout. But being a part of the fellows program has clearly affected him and how he sees himself in the world, having experienced it as a significant part of creating a loving community in the schools. His experience is a compelling argument for taking a new look at how we structure substitute teaching.

The Four Defining Characteristics of Substitute Teaching

Under-Resourced

First, there is the obvious: substitute teaching is dramatically under-resourced. Many leaders are hesitant to take a deep look at substitute teaching because they are under extreme pressure to make tight budgets work and assume any positive change will have a big price tag. Among the most frequent things we hear when we talk to people about substitute teaching is that the low pay is hugely limiting. There's a concept in design, borrowed from improv, which is often referred to as "yes, and . . ." where you build off insights, and recognize the importance of not shutting ideas down. Increasing sub pay is a "yes, and . . ." We don't think substitute teachers are paid enough. While we're on the subject, we don't think teachers are paid enough either. Nonetheless, we believe there are a number of things that can—and should—be done in conjunction with raising substitute pay that can have a significant impact on changing the experience for everyone involved. We start with these other, nonpay items because we have found that leading with the pay issue tends to shut down the discussion. Either people explain why they can't increase pay, or they increase pay and figure that should be enough to fix it.

Scale

Along with (and related to) the lack of resources, the sheer scale of substitute teaching makes it a difficult issue to work on. This makes everything harder, from the ability to offer professional development to the simple act of putting out communications. Imagine that you are the only person in your district working on substitute teaching

RETIRED TEACHER · WORKING ARTIST

and you put out an announcement to your pool of hundreds of subs. You are bound to get back questions, concerns, and suggestions in response. That volume can quickly become overwhelming, even if just a small percentage of subs engage with you. This shows up most clearly in decisions around investing in professional development for subs. The cost of paying subs to attend trainings adds up very quickly—a key reason they receive so little of it.

Variety

As you've already read, there is an incredible variety in the world of substitute teaching. From who subs are and what motivates them, to the variety of places and types of jobs they work in, it's difficult to express just how varied it is. This makes it tough to pinpoint potential changes for a larger system.

The disparate levels of subs' experience and preparation make it difficult to design PD and, from what we've seen, PD tends to be aimed at the lowest common denominator. It's hard to feel excited about offering PD that you know won't meet most peoples' needs.

It's also challenging that the same few people are responsible for the entire substitute teaching system—both short-term and long-term subs. The roles are very different, and lumping them together can make it hard to see opportunities for redesign. In our work we almost always narrow our focus, working specifically on short-term absences or new subs.

The Missing Manager

There are structural reasons why substitute teaching systems don't get a lot of focus. The biggest is something we've come to call the "missing manager." The only in-depth study of substitute teaching that we are aware of comes to the same conclusion, summarizing the takeaways in a now out-of-print book called *Effective Substitute Teachers: Myth, Mayhem or Magic (Roadmaps to Success)*. They state it succinctly: "the problems with substitute teacher programs were a result of nonmanagement rather than mismanagement."

Formally, human resources (HR) is responsible for hiring and managing substitute teachers. They play a traditional HR role, focused on recruitment, hiring, and formal discipline. HR would traditionally work hand in hand with a manager who would provide mentoring and guidance, helping a new employee to understand their job and how they fit into broader district goals. This function is missing for substitute teachers. Once hired, substitute teachers are largely on their own and may have little to no ongoing interaction with HR. They have no one to talk over issues or celebrate successes with, and no one to notice when they are struggling.

Typically, the sub coordinator is supervised by a certificated director—they are the person in charge of all HR matters for anyone whose position requires a credential. The certificated director is also responsible for teacher recruitment, retention, and discipline. These are some of the busiest people you'll meet. While they'd like to bring more attention and strategy to substitute teaching, their top priority

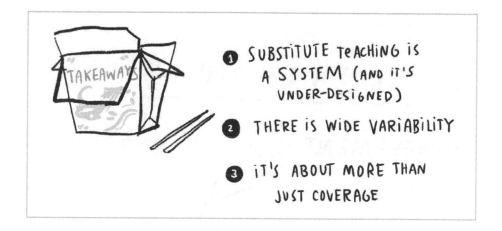

1. SUBSTITUTE TEACHING IS A SYSTEM (AND IT'S UNDER-DESIGNED)
2. THERE IS WIDE VARIABILITY
3. IT'S ABOUT MORE THAN JUST COVERAGE

has to be the permanent classroom teachers. This means that there is no leader with the bandwidth to work deeply on making substitute teaching work better.

Takeaways

- **Substitute Teaching is a (Under-designed) System:** Substitute teaching is a significant part of a student's educational experience that is woefully under-designed. The system might be invisible in some ways, but understanding the complexity of it explains why it can be hard to change.
- **There is Lots of Variation:** There is wide variability in the experience of substitute teaching—from short term to long term, subject area, elementary vs. high school, and requirements and pay.
- **It's About More than Coverage:** Substitute teaching is often measured in terms of coverage—i.e., the presence of a sub—which is generally uneven within a given district. Using coverage as the measure of substitute teaching also limits our expectations of the role by measuring the presence of a sub, as opposed to the quality of the experience.

Start Where You Are

Before we turn our attention to innovation—ideas for rethinking how substitute teaching works—we want to share what we've learned about making the current system work better. There is a blurry line between improvement and innovation, but we think of this chapter as focused squarely on improvement. How do you work within your current context to make substitute teaching work better? Think practical and actionable advice for busy leaders. If you are a sub, parent, partner, or other community member reading this book, we hope that it gives you a window into what it's like to hold these leadership roles, and some ideas for working with your own leaders.

In this chapter we draw on our research and on our experience with leaders at the school and district level. One of the most rewarding parts of the process is when we work side-by-side with these leaders to improve how substitute teaching functions in their school. It gives us a deeper understanding of how the system and the people within it operate today. Almost across the board, the principals we have worked with have been dedicated, creative, make-it-happen people. They are inspiring, and we are deeply motivated by the goal of making things work a little better for them. Ditto for office managers, assistant principals (APs), and teachers. We also enjoy the chance to work with human resources (HR) leaders. They are people-people who light up at the thought of helping someone along their path. Their knowledge of the employment side of education is staggering and, like the principals, they are masters of juggling tasks and getting things done. Their plates are almost always overflowing, but they want to make things work better for subs. Just like with principals, our team gets excited about helping these leaders reach their goals.

Let's dive in.

What Matters:
Subs Coming Back

If you are thinking about how to improve substitute teaching at your school or district, your strategy boils down to one question: how can we get subs to come back? We've now done hundreds of interviews with people connected to substitute teaching and collected hundreds of personal stories. They are as varied as the field, but every single positive story we've come across has one thing in common: they are about substitute teachers returning to a school over and over. These subs feel more connected and effective, and have a greater sense of the impact of their work. The day goes better for students because they know the sub; the adult in front of the class isn't a stranger. Teachers feel less anxious because they know the sub and, understandably, they tend to prepare better plans for subs they know.

In addition to it being a better experience for everyone involved, improving retention improves coverage. It also has the happy side effect of reducing the churn of subs coming in and out of a school or district. Less time is required to get new subs hired and up to speed, which means that leaders have more bandwidth to focus on efforts like building relationships with subs (and the hundred other things on their always-overflowing plate). Rather than the vicious

BUILDING RELATIONSHIPS

cycles we see in many areas of substitute teaching, focusing on repeat subs creates a virtuous cycle.

So how do you do it? First, let's turn our attention to why a sub might want to come back.

In *Drive: The Surprising Truth About What Motivates Us*, Daniel Pink identifies three factors for motivation at work: autonomy, mastery, and purpose. We love this framework for thinking about substitute teaching, and have tweaked it slightly to mesh with our learnings. While people are often drawn to substitute teaching because of the autonomy—choose your own schedule, no manager directing your work—in our interviews we hear a deep need for community. Subs often feel isolated—surrounded by students but, like Joyce in our opening story, held at arm's length by the adults with whom they work. So we modify Pink's framework, replacing *autonomy* with *community*. We have also reframed Pink's emphasis on *purpose* to focus instead on *meaning*. Our experience is that while purpose isn't always apparent, meaning can always be made.

A quick definition of each:

- **Meaning:** The feeling that your work matters, that you are making a positive contribution to society. For example, substitute teachers will often tell us stories about times when they felt like they made a connection with a student who was struggling, and offered advice they thought helped. In our interviews we've noticed that subs also have a desire for other people to acknowledge that their work matters: it's frustrating to feel like you are making a difference but that your successes are invisible.
- **Mastery:** The feeling that you are getting better at something. Pink gives the example of learning an instrument, and describes how the experience of mastering a new skill is motivating. Substitute teaching has a steep learning curve. From figuring out how to introduce yourself to a new class to crafting the perfect fill-in activity, subs learn how to do the job while they're on the job. In our interviews, subs often light up when they describe all they've learned since they started.
- **Community:** A big part of feeling motivated is feeling like you have a professional community. Not just people who smile and say hello, but people who know you and care about you. The feeling of professional isolation can be overwhelming for substitute teachers. When we pull together groups for trainings, often we find that what subs really want and need is to share their experience and feel heard by their colleagues.

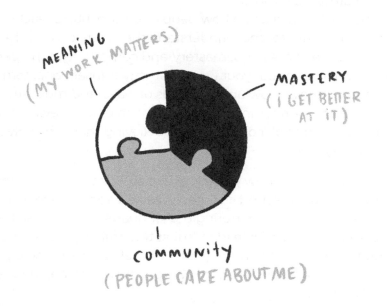

MEANING
(MY WORK MATTERS)

MASTERY
(I GET BETTER AT IT)

COMMUNITY
(PEOPLE CARE ABOUT ME)

This simple framework helps us think about how to increase the likelihood that a substitute teacher returns. If we can increase the experiences of meaning, mastery, and community, we help subs feel a greater sense of satisfaction and motivation. In short, this framework gives us a roadmap for how to make substitute teaching a better job. If we can make it a better job, subs will come back, which is better for everyone.

Language Matters

Before we dig into school and district level strategies, we want you to reflect on how you talk about substitute teachers today. Whatever role you are in, you have a big impact on how people see substitute teachers and how substitute teachers understand their own jobs. It is hard to invite a sense of meaning, mastery, and community if the people you work with talk about your work in strictly transactional terms. Transactional terms show up in all kinds of ways, and most are dehumanizing, like referring to subs as "warm bodies," evaluating everything in terms of "coverage," and believing that subs only show up for the paycheck.

One easy way to shift how you talk about subs is to consider how the language would sound if someone talked about teachers in the same way. Consider mirroring the language that you use for teachers. For example, instead of "substitute training," refer to it as "sub professional development (PD)." This helps to send the signal—to everyone—that subs are a core part of how instruction happens, and a place to invest.

What's in a Name?

One of the innovations we've seen districts adopt is essentially a rebranding of subs as "guest instructors" or "guest teachers." In general, we think this is a great idea. The very idea of there being a "substitute" for a classroom teacher strikes us as strange. It's alienating for the classroom teacher, and not particularly helpful for the person being asked to fill the classroom teacher's shoes. A word of warning, though: when we interviewed subs in a local district about their reactions to being called "guest instructors" instead of "subs," there was a healthy skepticism around rebranding the position without changing the experience.

Building Relationships at the School Level

Most schools are already working to build and maintain relationships with substitute teachers. The most common way this shows up is when schools maintain a short list of substitute  teachers who work frequently at their school. This is an example of the informal system for getting subs into assignments.

We talked about this a bit in the last chapter, and it's an important concept to note. In considering how to best build relationships with subs, it's important to acknowledge that there are really two different systems that exist for getting subs: formal and informal. The informal one works better, and is more likely to get repeat subs. The formal system is characterized by a centralized pool, into which teachers put job requests, and subs sign up to fill them. In the informal system, schools have a shortlist of subs they've gotten to know, and they call them before the job is ever put into the system. Often it is the individual teacher who has the relationship with the individual sub, but in many schools, the school secretary develops a network as well. In either case, the informal system is built on social capital or, more specifically, personal relationships. When there is significant teacher (or principal) turnover, one of the many negative consequences that contributes to even greater disruption is that social capital can be lost.

Where this is working, we observe that the principal sees it as their job to build and steward the shortlist of preferred subs. For example, Principal Burnham describes her relationship with a frequent sub: "I've been able to build a relationship with a retired teacher who gets what we are trying to get done for our students and wants to be a part of it. He knows whatever class he's in, even if there are challenges, I am right there to help. That's why he keeps coming back." When principals support staff in these ways, the percentage of jobs entered into the sub assignment system as "pre-arranged" increases. Dedicating ongoing time to building this list is important because subs—especially the good ones—often transition to other jobs.

It's also important that principal leadership in this area be expressed out loud and that you engage your staff in the process. Often teachers will have strong relationships with individual subs—the sub will feel comfortable working for Ms. Green, but doesn't know Mr. Lyon next door. It's great that Ms. Green has this relationship, but your goal is for the sub to feel comfortable stepping into any of your classrooms, and you need Ms. Green to feel appreciated for bringing this important resource into your school.

Building Your Sub Shortlist

If you don't already have a shortlist, here's a quick summary of how it works.

When a substitute teacher has had a good day at your school, ask them if they'd like to work there again. If they agree, get their contact information (*make sure this includes both cell phone numbers and email addresses*). Typically, the list is maintained by the school secretary or office manager—whoever is in charge of monitoring the sub assignment system and greeting subs in the morning. When a job comes up, the school secretary might call those subs first and ask if they are available before putting the job in the system, where any sub can pick it up. We usually see these handwritten lists posted near the office manager's desk, often accompanied by scribbled notes like "doesn't like kindergarten" or "can't do Wednesdays" in the margins. In our experience, a mid-sized elementary school should aim to have six to eight subs on their list.

If you haven't previously maintained a list, this single practice will make a big difference!

Beyond recruitment, adopting schoolwide practices around subs can have a significant impact on improving not only your coverage rates, but the quality of the subs you attract and retain. One of the least considered and most important ways to elevate the sub experience is shifting sub prep from an individualized practice to a schoolwide practice by instituting clear templates that all teachers use, and setting aside collaboration time to work together on things like emergency plans.

Sub Plans, Every Time

Perhaps one of the most important things we've heard from subs, if not *the* most important thing, is that there need to be sub plans every time. To say the least, it is highly memorable when subs don't get them. In an "I'm never going back" kind of way. After creating a sub list, this is the thing that we recommend school leaders focus on next.

We've learned a lot about sub plans in the last few years. One of the most striking things is just how different plans look from teacher to teacher. That's because at most schools, sub prep is an individual practice—something teachers do on their own. Not surprisingly, some teachers are better than others at writing directions for adults. It's worth noting here that new teachers need help creating plans because no one covers this in credentialing programs. No, really—we've asked. So as you bring increased focus to substitute teaching, we recommend you take a look at what plans really look like. It's critical to provide subs with comprehensive plans that are easy to understand and implement; these plans are key elements in getting subs to come back.

We also see a remarkable difference when there is a clear process for putting that plan into the subs' hands (some of the most disheartening stories we hear are subs who find plans at the end of the day—"... and then I lifted up the bin and there were the plans!"). School secretaries are the ones who usually end up fielding these interactions, so making the process clearer qualitatively improves their day,

and encourages them to take more leadership and responsibility in building supportive relationships with preferred subs. Finally, it's important to signal to subs that they can count on receiving a plan at your school. We've seen that including a note in the sub request that says something like "look for plans in the bright pink binder" makes a difference in how quickly (or if) the job is picked up.

Requiring teachers to leave plans sounds pretty straightforward, and it's one of those issues that is easily minimized as a function of compliance. Flipping this, and trying to understand why teachers sometimes don't leave plans, is helpful in effectively redesigning the system. Imagine you're a teacher. You work hard at creating a robust plan, but then the sub doesn't use the plan or, worse, no sub shows up. It's demoralizing. The next time you're going to be out, it's hard to motivate yourself. You put in a half-hearted effort, which in turn gets a half-hearted response from the sub. In short order, it's not hard to imagine how a teacher might decide not to leave a plan. What's easy to lose sight of if you are the teacher in this scenario, is how this issue is at the heart of the vicious cycle that exacerbates low coverage. Teachers at schools with low coverage are discouraged by creating plans that never get used, so they stop making plans. When a sub does show up, there isn't a plan, and then they never come back, causing the coverage to sink even lower. The only thing that we have found that helps in addressing a vicious cycle is remembering that a virtuous cycle is just the pattern in reverse; you can have a tremendous amount of influence on causing the tides to shift.

Build Schoolwide Practices

Our goal is to deepen the relationship between your school and your favorite subs. One way to do this is to bring more consistency to how teachers prepare for subs and what subs are asked to do with students. The more you can create schoolwide practices, the more comfortable subs will be stepping into any classroom, and not just for the teachers they know. Adopting schoolwide practices around subs can have a significant impact on improving not only your coverage rates, but the quality of the subs you attract and retain.

A Shift in Narrative

There's also a role for students in shifting schoolwide practices. As it stands, the shared narrative around subs is generally unkind. The unspoken expectation is that students are going to behave badly and treat the sub disrespectfully. On one level, this seems fairly benign, in the spirit of "we were terrible to subs when we were kids, it's always been this way," etc. On the other hand, when you realize this sets kids up to be disrespectful to complete strangers visiting their school—people who are guests in their classroom, there to keep them safe and, in an ideal world, even teach them some stuff—it seems like a pretty messed up thing to teach our kids.

Consistent Systems

Simple, schoolwide expectations that remain consistent as students move up through the grades can begin to shift this narrative. It can be hard for a teacher to articulate their classroom management system for a sub, but a simple system that is used every time there is a sub, and that students learn over time in every

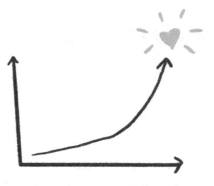

class, clarifies expectations and improves communication among everyone involved.

Building on these expectations with a core set of activities that students do with subs makes it even more automatic. One of our favorites is the sub interview: students prepare interview questions and an interview protocol in advance of the teacher's absence. They then conduct the interview as an opening activity when a sub visits. It's an excellent opportunity to do some applied social emotional learning. Along these same lines, our friends at the Center for Collaborative Classrooms have a whole week-long set of activities around preparing for a sub in the second edition of their Caring School Community curriculum. They start the unit with a class meeting, and we've included the lesson from their first edition in the Resources chapter.

Buddy Teachers

Many schools have a "buddy teacher" system in place. If you do, make sure that you have taken the time to establish shared expectations for what happens when there is a substitute teacher. As you read in the opening story, having a teacher check in on the sub can make a big difference in their day. One of the things subs worry—and tell war stories—about is sending a student to the office because of behavioral issues only to have them sent back to class. If you have an alternative, like sending them to a buddy teacher class, make sure that system is in place and is clear to the sub.

Small Things that Make a Difference

Before we leave this topic, we wanted to include a handful of small things that we've seen work for schools.

Orient Subs to Your School

It may seem like a small gesture, but an effort to help the sub get oriented can go a long way. Imagine you are arriving at your school for the first time. Is it obvious where you should park? Is the street address different than where the entrance to the building is? Would you know where to find the bathroom? Where to eat lunch? This even includes things like where to put one's purse or other belongings, lunch availability. Precisely because these become second nature to us when we work at the same place every day, we often forget to convey them, and it can reinforce a sub's sense of being "other." Creating a welcome sheet to give to new subs reduces confusion and helps a sub know how things work at your school. If it's particularly confusing to find your school entrance or parking, include these things in the notes on sub requests. These gestures not only help subs have a less stressful arrival and set them up for a more successful day overall, they send a signal that this is a school that takes good care of its subs.

Regular Emails

Another effort that goes a long way in helping subs feel more connected to your school is to send them a few notes throughout the year. That's why we suggest collecting their email addresses. You don't need to make it complicated; a simple note before Thanksgiving that says, "Thanks for subbing at our school. I am thankful to have wonderful subs like you. Have a restful and rejuvenating Thanksgiving break—see you in December!" can help a sub feel recognized. It also nudges them to come back to your school during the winter, which is usually a heavier absence period. The meaning–mastery–community framework can be a helpful tool to use as you're thinking about what to write in these messages.

Invite to Events

To help subs feel connected to the community you are creating around your students, invite them to your community events. Things like a back-to-school night, family science night, or your school carnival can be very meaningful events for subs to be part of. If you have staff potlucks or teacher appreciation events, it's also really nice to include your most frequent subs in these types of gathering.

Admittedly, this can be a bit complicated because of pay. If you have the ability to pay your most frequent subs to attend a few school events, that's great. But if you don't, consider inviting them with a note that says something to the effect of "You are an important part of our school community and I wanted to personally invite you to this event. This is an uncompensated event for staff."

Quick Ideas for Building a Sense of Meaning, Mastery, and Community

Meaning:

- Tell your subs how they contribute to what you are trying to get done for your students.
- If you hear that a sub connected with a student in a positive way, share that back with them.
- Subs often don't know why the teacher is absent. If appropriate, share how they have enabled a teacher to do something important—to deepen their skills through PD, take care of their family, or take care of themselves.

Mastery:

- Offer subs feedback and note their progress.
- Give concrete suggestions.
- Ask about their personal goals—are they aspiring teachers? If so, they might appreciate the opportunity to teach a real lesson. In our workshops, aspiring teachers are sometimes shy about engaging with principals.

Community:

- Invite subs to school community events.
- Consider inviting frequent subs to your school PD activities.
- If you have a staff board with photos, consider including frequent subs.
- School swag goes a long way! Giving a t-shirt or lanyard can make subs feel like part of the team.

Why Focus on It?
It Works

We hope these ideas spark your own ideas for deepening your relationship with subs. One question we sometimes get from principals is: "Why should I focus on this? Isn't substitute teaching a district-level responsibility?" Before we turn to the district level, we wanted to take a moment to talk directly about this because we suspect some version of this question might be lingering in your mind.

The most important thing to say here is: it works. School-level practices matter, and we know from first-hand experience that they make a difference, even in the most dire of sub situations. If you have less than half of sub requests covered today and are convinced that subs just don't want to come to your school, trust us when we say these simple strategies work. We know because we've worked side-by-side with school teams as they implemented them. It's not magic—it's just about putting more attention on a problem. And if you are experiencing many unstaffed days, you are already spending a lot of time on this problem. It's worth investing some on building relationships with subs.

One other practical thing to say here: as you read in the last chapter, one of the defining characteristics of substitute teaching is the missing manager. In most places, there isn't anyone focused on sub strategy. Our conversations with superintendents usually boil down to something like "substitute teaching is on our priority list, but it's never going to be at the top." It is a classic example of the system breakdown that can happen when the decision-making body is removed from the actual team experiencing the pain point. Given this, our advice to principals is generally not to wait for system-level change. The reality is that if substitute teaching isn't going well at your school, it's taking a ton of your time and it's making it tough to advance the rest of your priorities. Perhaps most importantly, it's a huge part of your students' experience of school.

Building Relationships at the District Level

For HR teams, we've seen that shifting from a focus on recruitment to a focus on retention can be transformative. Substitute teaching is often a transitional role, so we aren't suggesting that you will retain all subs for the long term. But shifting your focus to building relationships with substitute teachers and helping them feel connected and supported will extend how often, and for how long, subs work for you.

It's also more rewarding for you. Many leaders we work with are exhausted by the constant churn, and emotionally drained by dealing with discipline issues all day. We've seen that for HR leaders we work with, focusing on building relationships helps to reconnect them with the part of HR work they find most motivating—helping people along their professional journey.

Let Data Guide You

Substitute assignment platforms create a record of every single substitute teaching day, resulting in a rich data set that can help guide your work, allowing you to focus in on which schools need the most help and which subs work most often. For example, when we looked at the data for one district, it turned out that 20% of their sub pool worked 80% of jobs. They had a large pool of subs who worked infrequently. Digging into the reasons behind why this was happening helped them craft their strategy; they focused on helping these more infrequent subs become more connected with schools.

At a minimum, we recommend actively tracking and widely sharing data that looks at:

- The number of jobs on an average day and average coverage rate.
- Coverage by school.
- Percentage of jobs filled by various methods.
- How often individual subs are working— average days/sub.

Working with Outsourcers

For HR leaders working with an outsourcing company, the challenges can be a little different. We strongly recommend:

- Ask for your stats on at least a semester basis—monthly is even better.
- Be sure to get the school-by-school breakdown.
- If you have schools that are under-served (and chances are you do) ask for a plan for addressing this.
- Require some training—make sure subs aren't charged for it.
- Ask for authority to communicate directly with substitute teachers.
- Ask for onsite recruitment events.

Substantial Classrooms: Redesigning the Substitute Teaching Experience

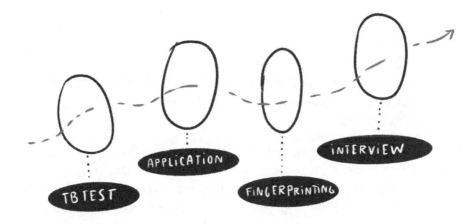

A Great First Experience

Your relationship with substitute teachers begins with their application and hiring process. If these are bad experiences for subs, it's very difficult to establish a positive relationship later. In almost every district we've worked with, there is significant work to do in these areas. It's quite difficult for you to see where improvements are needed because you are deep in the process yourself. If you do it every single day, the process probably makes sense to you. You know the steps and what needs to happen to keep someone moving forward through the process. You also have the technical knowledge about things like how permits work and what documents are needed. But for a sub going through it for the first time, it might not be as clear.

Our advice is to find someone you trust who doesn't currently work in education and ask them to apply to be a substitute teacher in your district. Ask them to journal their experience, writing down what questions they had, where they looked for answers, and what was confusing. Use a journey map to get a better understanding of what it felt like for them. Speaking from experience, there is always room to improve these types of processes, so push yourself to listen for places of confusion, and try to use a fresh perspective to make your directions more accessible. Follow this all the way through your onboarding process.

We start here because not only is this the beginning of your relationship with subs, it's also likely the place you are spending most of your time. If you can streamline this process and reduce the number of questions you are fielding, you will have more time to invest in building relationships with subs. If you don't create more room on your plate, it's very difficult to add anything.

Professional Development for Subs

Seen through the meaning–mastery–community framework, PD is a key opportunity to help substitute teachers feel more engaged and motivated in their work, and one of the best ways for districts to deepen their relationship with the substitute teachers in their pool. Every HR leader we've encountered wants to offer more PD for subs, but as we discussed in the last chapter, budget constraints make this challenging.

One outside resource that many districts rely upon for professional development is Utah State's Substitute Teaching Institute, STEDI. Founded in 1995, STEDI.org provides training materials and services and has spearheaded much of the research that exists around recruiting, training, and retention efforts in the field.

We've also seen HR leaders successfully leverage their internal resources to address the professional development challenge by reaching out to the teams who work on professional development for teachers. Express your interest in getting subs more PD and start them thinking about the question. If your district provides online PD or other resources for teachers, ask if substitute teachers can also access these resources. At a minimum, work with these instructional leaders to create your own resource page for substitute teachers, and link to open-source materials that will help them gain familiarity with your core curriculum.

As we also mentioned above, there are some negative and deep-seated narratives about substitute teachers. Your goal is to encourage instructional leaders to increasingly think of substitutes as teachers. After all, subs are how 10% of instruction happens in your district. Be intentional about mirroring the language used for teachers—e.g., instead of "training" for subs, use "PD" for subs. It also helps to be polite yet explicit about the types of learning experiences you want to create for substitute teachers. You want to use best practices for adult learning: less "sit and get" and more experiential and activity-based instruction, with significant opportunities for peer feedback and connection.

Subs love to learn from each other; asking a substitute teacher to share their learning with their colleagues helps to build their own sense of mastery and community. As Amaris Johnson, sub specialist in Arlington Public Schools explains, "subs value learning from each other, it's the thing they most appreciate in our sub professional learning events. Experienced subs want to share their tips and new subs want to learn from people who've been there." Arlington Public Schools host an annual Back to Subbing event in parallel with the back-to-school PD that happens at schools.

Encourage Relationships with Schools

We know that subs are more likely to persist if they have relationships with a few schools. It's worth thinking about how you might encourage these relationships, especially for new subs. This is a delicate balance; subs value their ability to choose where and when they work. But it's also overwhelming to look at a long list of sub jobs on a computer screen and try to figure out where to go. It's not surprising that subs usually go to places that feel familiar and comfortable.

One of our favorite strategies for encouraging relationships between subs and schools is a "new sub tour." Here's how it works: invite new subs to join you for a morning visit to three or four schools. At each school, arrange for the principal to give subs a tour of their school and talk about what it's like to work there. This can help dispel myths about certain schools and jumpstarts relationship building between subs and those schools. This also subtly nudges school teams to focus on what substitute teachers need to feel welcome and supported.

Additionally, and to this end, taking the time to interview school staff—either the principal or the office manager, or both—can help you get a better understanding of the system you manage from their perspective. Diving into their stories and seeking to understand what the world looks like from their perspective can help reframe problems, leading to new insights and opportunities.

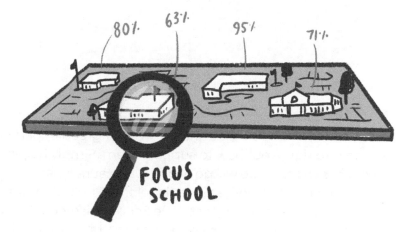

COVERAGE

80% 63% 95% 71%

FOCUS SCHOOL

Focus Schools

As we talked about in the last chapter, the scale of substitute teaching can make it difficult to focus on relationship building. That's true both for supporting individual subs, and helping schools improve their practices and build relationships with subs. When we work in larger systems with dozens—or hundreds—of schools, we suggest the strategy of focusing on the schools that need the most support. We call this the "focus school strategy." Here's how it works.

Start with your current coverage rates for all schools. Chances are there is significant disparity between your highest and lowest coverage schools. Identify the 5–10 lowest coverage schools and invite them to participate in an opt-in program to get additional support from HR. Since you will be working on changing school practices—a.k.a. asking them to do work—we think it's important to make this opt-in. Schools have lots of priorities and you are looking for those that believe this is a top priority. We often suggest that HR teams focus on elementary schools because, as you read, the practice of farming out students has a big learning impact on a large number of students.

Once you've identified the schools and they have agreed to partici-pate, your job is to figure out how to support them. Simply helping them bring focus to this issue will go a long way. Laura Kaiser, director of Talent Support Services in Philadelphia Public Schools, explains how this works in her district: "The School District of Phila-delphia's Substitute Services Team conducts monthly calls with high priority schools. This allows Talent to understand what's happening on the ground so they can better support school leadership in iden-tifying and implementing solutions. Principals have noted that they appreciate Talent's effort to get involved. The Substitute Services Team also works closely with Talent Partners (who support princi-pals on their staffing issues) to ensure their efforts are aligned and strategic."

Focusing on the schools that are struggling the most will help you to provide more personal and meaningful support. Principals appre-ciate that HR is making the effort, and the HR team has a better understanding of what's happening on the ground. We've also helped schools strengthen their systems for creating and managing sub plans (as you'll read in the Design Lab chapter, we've now built an online platform for this). If you are considering adding something like school tours to introduce subs to individual schools, it works well to bring them to focus schools.

Small Things that Make a Difference

Before we leave this topic, we wanted to share a few other small practices that we've seen make a difference. They closely parallel what we suggested for principals.

Regular Communications

We are surprised by how often we find that HR teams have no ongoing communication with subs. If you want substitute teachers to feel committed to your district, it's important to send them regular communications. We recommend keeping it simple; just four to six notes through the school year. The easiest way to start is with seasonal notes at five key points: welcome back to school, appreciation at Thanksgiving, welcome back from winter break, Substitute Teacher Appreciation Day (1st week of May), and wish them a good summer at the end of the school year.

Appreciation Event

Another HR-led activity that we've seen work well is an annual appreciation for subs. It doesn't have to be an event—it could be everyone in HR signing thank you cards once a year. Some districts ask principals to "nominate" outstanding subs. You can also jump on the Sub Appreciation Week bus, which occurs during the first week in May every year. If your district has a social media person, coordinate with them for Sub Appreciation Week and make sure you have sample posts for your principals to put on Facebook.

Shadowing

We'll end with what might be the simplest, but can also be the most powerful, suggestion: a shadow day. We know, we know—you're ridiculously busy. But spending a day shadowing a sub can be eye-opening and transformative—for you, for your school board members, for your principals, for your superintendent. When in doubt, more empathy is always a good answer.

Takeaways

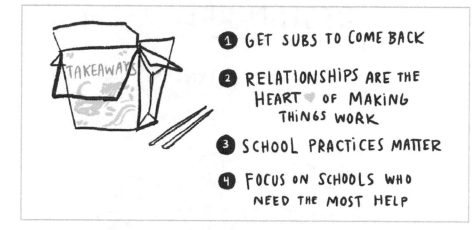

1. GET SUBS TO COME BACK
2. RELATIONSHIPS ARE THE HEART ♥ OF MAKING THINGS WORK
3. SCHOOL PRACTICES MATTER
4. FOCUS ON SCHOOLS WHO NEED THE MOST HELP

- **Retention is Key.** When in doubt, focus on getting the subs you already have to come back.
- **Relationships are at the Heart of Making Things Work.** Whether it is the relationship between a school and a sub or an HR director and a school, investing in the care and feeding of these relationships makes all the difference, especially when things get hard.
- **School Practices Matter.** Subs go back to schools where they have a good experience and a lot of that is about how schools prepare for and support subs. Schoolwide practices help you bring more consistency to what happens when a sub is on campus.
- **Start with the Schools Who Need the Most Help.** In every district there are schools with higher and lower coverage. Focus on those with the lowest coverage, put your energy in the places it matters most.

DESIGN LAB

IMPROVEMENT   INNOVATION

IT'S A FUZZY LINE!

IT FELT LIKE...

THEN I...

INTERVIEWS & OBSERVATION

PROTOTYPE & TEST

Design Lab

Welcome to Substantial's Design Lab! While our last chapter was focused on improvement—how you can make the current system work better—this chapter encourages you to imagine a different future for substitute teaching. We warmly invite you to join us in this work.

In this chapter we'll introduce you to the basics of design thinking and share some of what we've learned about using this approach. Design is best learned through doing, so we want to give you enough in this chapter to get started, but it's hard to convey the magic of design thinking in writing. You've got to try it to understand it.

Keep in mind that design thinking is more art than science. Don't worry about doing it right—there isn't a "right." Just make sure to start with interviews and observations that can help you deeply understand people's lived experience (a.k.a. build empathy), and test ideas quickly in the real world. These two practices get you most of the way there! We are going to share the tools and mindset tips that we have found most useful for putting these two ideas—"work from empathy" and "test in the real world"—into practice.

What Is Design Thinking?

The term "design thinking" refers to the framework, process, and mindsets that designers use to create new things, usually new products. One of the fundamental attributes of design work is that you can't see the destination when you start: you don't get a blueprint for what you are building. Designers must rely on a process for how they find inspiration, develop ideas, and ultimately create something that hadn't been previously imagined. Over the last few decades, that process and its accompanying mindsets have come to be called design thinking, and have been applied in all sorts of different settings.

Doing design work—the work of imagining something new into the world—requires you to wade into the unknown. On our team we sometimes talk about it as wading into a thick fog. It can be a very disorienting experience: you can't yet see where you are going, and you need to have faith in the process to guide you forward. It's not a linear path, and there are often profound moments of disequilibrium along the way. But as you progress, the emerging picture becomes more clear.

Lucky for us, other designers have waded into the fog before us, and are willing to teach us what they know about how to navigate through it.

Learn More

There is a culture of openness—sharing what you know—among designers, which means there are tons of resources to help you learn about design thinking. Since some of the earliest thinking about Substantial was done while Jill was at Stanford's Hasso Plattner Institute of Design (the d.school), we are partial to the brand of design thinking the d.school has been promoting for almost 20 years. If you are looking to learn more about the design thinking process, we strongly recommend that you start with their website. We've included a curated list of some of our favorite resources in the Resources chapter at the end of the book.

Substantial Classrooms: Redesigning the Substitute Teaching Experience

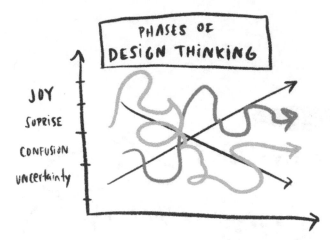

Doing Design Work—Our Basic Cycle

While we encourage you to learn more about design thinking from the experts, we wanted to include our basic design cycle. We've simplified the classic process, focusing especially on early empathy work and testing in the real world. Having just four steps to keep track of helps us incorporate design into every part of our work. Think of it less as a formal process and more like a guiding framework.

Here's how it works. We start with empathy work, doing interviews and observations. This empathy work generates insights, new ways of understanding the challenge and what is needed. These insights drive us to come up with new ideas to meet that need, and we quickly move to prototype and test one. Testing with people, in real settings as often as possible, kicks off a new cycle of empathy–insight–making–testing. Moving through these cycles quickly, we mothball ideas that don't work (basically setting them aside) and refine those that show promise. Each experiment adds to our understanding of the dynamics at play, and we often bring back mothballed ideas, combining them with new insights to try them again.

While this process might sound linear, like a sequence of steps, it can feel quite messy. We've found that creating processes and rituals helps us move through the work. One thing you notice when you spend time with professional designers like our friends at the d.school is that they are very quick to action. If you are used to working in a more analytically focused culture, this can feel uncomfortable. We invite you to push through that feeling and start testing things in small ways as soon as possible. You will learn more and create more momentum.

We've learned that each phase has a different energy. Some feel exciting, others disorienting. Some require focus, while others require you to think more expansively. Having a sense of what energy to expect helps us to ride those waves, and is part of how the framework is internalized. During certain parts of the process you can expect to feel different things. If you aren't experiencing a range of emotions, uneasiness, and frustration, it's a good sign that you aren't being true to the process—you might be just walking through the motions rather than really committing to the creative work. (Sounds great, doesn't it?)

Let's take a closer look at each step.

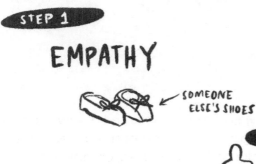

STEP 1

EMPATHY

SOMEONE ELSE'S SHOES

1. Empathy

INTERVIEW, OBSERVATION, RESEARCH

All of our most powerful insights have come from getting to know people connected to substitute teaching. This connection is also what gives our team the emotional energy needed to kick off a project and stick with it. Substitute teaching is a deeply human endeavor, but it's often thought of in transactional terms, or in the abstract at the policy level.

If you are used to starting with analysis, starting with empathy can feel revelatory. Instead of trying to comprehensively understand a problem, you zoom in on just a handful of people and places. If you do this with a sense of curiosity and openness, it's amazing how quickly you will unearth both the key dynamics at play and new ways to understand the challenge. (In the Design Playbook we've included a few techniques for early empathy work: interviews, observation, and the card sort.)

Empathy is also essential for working on a system as multifaceted as substitute teaching. There are so many different types of people, with different types of backgrounds, working in different types of schools, in different types of assignments. While you can imagine improvements to the current system that might have near universal appeal—like raising pay—it's more challenging to find innovative ideas that meet the whole system's needs. To this end, we are searching for the unexpected insight that leads us to new ideas.

From the relative serenity of our office we might look at survey data and dispassionately note that subs don't always receive plans and, as a result, sometimes they need to wing it. We may know this is a potential problem, but our understanding of that problem is at a surface level and, to be honest, our ideas about how to address it would be too. As we talk to teachers, we begin to understand why this might happen. Behind each missing plan is a story, and each story helps us have more empathy for the teacher. Maybe no sub showed up the last three times they requested a sub, and they decided it wasn't worth the time to prepare a plan that wasn't going to be used. Or maybe their daughter has been in and out of hospital this month and they've used up all of their just-in-case plans. None of this is visible from the data, and if we only asked in general about their consistency in leaving plans for subs, every teacher would answer "always." We also wouldn't see the sub who creates his own go-to activities (his favorite is helping kindergarteners write and per-form a play) when he finds himself without plans.

Thinking about the teacher with the sick daughter or the one who's tired of wasting time changes your understanding of the challenge. Starting with people puts a human face on the thing you are working on, and instead of wanting to make it work better in the abstract, you want to be creative about making it work better for a specific person. Going out and talking with people and observing how things work in the real world changes how we understand what is needed.

Wondering how many people you need to talk to? It's fewer than you think. Our general rule is that three people/places can give you a good sense of the dynamics and enough inspiration to drive you to your first prototype. If we don't see clear themes emerging from three, we some-times do another round of interviews and observations. But most of the time three is more than enough. Yes, there is the risk that the folks that you interviewed have very specific experiences and the insights you gather won't be universal enough. But the great thing about using a design thinking methodology is that you move very quickly to testing ideas. If you've created a thing that doesn't resonate with other people, you mothball that idea and move on. The stakes for getting it right are low because you are going to move very quickly to validating your insights, and will learn if you are focusing on a niche problem.

2. Insight

Once we've done this early empathy work, the next step is making meaning of what we saw and heard. It's very tempting to jump to solutions, but the step of reflecting on what you heard helps you go deeper toward understanding the real needs, and often leads to an "a-ha" moment that helps you frame the problem in a different way.

This step forces you to slow down and sit with what you observed. It's tough to do alone, which is part of why design thinking is usually highly collaborative. There is no science to making meaning, and there is no right answer. It can feel frustratingly squishy, but what you are doing is looking for an insight that feels significant. Again, don't worry—the stakes are low! The power of design thinking comes in validating your insights quickly with low-cost, rapid testing.

"A-ha" moments can come at any time, like while you are taking a shower, making breakfast, or going on a walk. But there are some techniques that can help you and your team make meaning together. The first is to debrief together about what you saw and heard, while trying to be as vivid as possible. Pay close attention to the things that surprised you—the contradictions and unlikely turns of phrase. In this step we also look for things that have emotional res-onance—comments, looks, interactions that stay with us. We like to do this with sticky notes, quickly putting notes up on a board or wall to record all that we saw. Something about stepping back, rearrang-ing the Post-its, and making connections as a group, can help your brain to see patterns and bring forth that elusive moment of clarity.

You end this step with a new framing of your problem. At this point you are still working hard to resist the urge to jump to a solution, so make sure that your framing of the problem isn't actually a solution in disguise. One technique that's helpful is to ask, "How Might We . . ." This phrasing helps to frame a question that can have multiple possible answers. (See the Design Playbook for more on creating great "How Might We . . ." questions.)

3. Create

If we were drawing out the design process in more detail, we might break this down into two steps. But in practice they often blend together, especially when you are actively working on an idea. In this step, you come up with many possible answers to your "How Might We . . ." question (the ideal number is more than you can possibly imagine you need) and then decide on one to prototype. Again, resist the urge to jump to an idea without generating a big list of possibilities. Coming up with many possible answers will push you to think beyond your first few ideas into territory that you hadn't thought of before. In the Design Playbook we've included some techniques for idea generation—a process that's sometimes referred to as "ideation."

Once you've landed on an idea to pursue, your job is to get that idea out of your head and into a form with which someone can interact. This is called a prototype: a physical representation of an idea. Early on, your prototypes should be fast and low-cost, things you could make in less than an hour, and preferably in less than 15 min. The goal is to construct just enough to convey the idea. In fact, if you make them too polished you won't get as much feedback; people don't want to criticize things that look like they required a huge amount of effort. Making something kind of "jenky" (yes, this is an actual word in the urban dictionary) invites people in to improve and co-create with you.

As you refine an idea your prototypes become more sophisticated, until finally they are ready for prime time. We share a practical description of the process in the Journey of an Idea section below.

4. Test with People

The next step is to test your prototype with the people you envision will ultimately be using it. Testing doesn't mean explaining your idea. It means watching them interact with your prototype without your framing or directions. That means if you are creating something you think a teacher would use, you'll need to find a teacher. Observing them interacting with your prototype and talking with them about it starts you on a new cycle. You are back to empathy, which will reveal new insights, leading to new ideas about how to meet the need, and a new or refined prototype to test. As you refine ideas, your prototypes become more sophisticated and your tests are closer and closer to being ready for real settings. We've described this in the Journey of an Idea section below as well.

The logistics of testing with people in work settings can be challenging. It's essential that you do everything you can to test in real settings. With substitute teaching we are usually focused on things that happen in a school, so we push to test in school settings. This way, you'll gain a better sense of the context in which your thing will be used—you'll see the secretary interrupted by a student needing a Bandaid, and the principal keeping her ear to the walkie-talkie. Early on, you'll be leaning on friends and personal networks to find testing sites—our earliest version of SubPlans was tested by Amanda's son's teacher after school (we did this in only 20 min). We've included some more tips about gathering feedback throughout this process in the Design Playbook.

KEY MINDSETS

1. BIAS TOWARDS ACTION

2. SHOW > TELL

3. EMBRACE EXPERIMENTATION

4. FOCUS ON HUMAN VALUES

5. CRAFT CLARITY

6. BE MINDFUL AS PROCESS

   FLARE   FOCUS

7. RADICAL COLLABORATION

   AWESOME THING!

Key Mindsets

Here's our take on the mindsets that the d.school calls out as being essential to effective design.

Bias Toward Action

While the synthesis process does require time and patience, the design process is oriented toward adopting constraints that compel you to actually try to do things, as opposed to endlessly perfecting things.

Show Don't Tell

Time and time again, we have found that having something physical to share (PowerPoint presentations don't count) changes how people interact with our ideas, and shifts their imaginations in a way that makes them more receptive, open to engaging with the ideas, and more likely to build on the ideas . . . even to the point of becoming invested in the ideas' success.

Embrace Experimentation

We think about embracing experimentation as the addendum to the Show Don't Tell mindset. It's a reminder that actually trying things—building the prototype or acting out the process—is a super-important part of how you learn.

Focus on Human Values

We tend to think of focusing on human values as another way of saying that how people feel matters. Having empathy for the people you are designing for, really listening to them, and then demonstrably incorporating their feedback, goes a long way. Not only does this help them feel like they are seen, heard, and valued—it's also critical to coming up with the best ideas.

Craft Clarity

We are huge fans of the Oliver Wendell Holmes quote, "For the simplicity on this side of complexity, I wouldn't give you a fig. But for the simplicity on the other side of complexity, for that I would give you anything I have." Crafting clarity is all about taking something messy and getting deep enough into it that you can pull out the core insight that inspires others. It's not like you really wanted a fig in the first place.

Be Mindful of Process

The design process can also be experienced as an alternating experience of flaring and focusing. In the empathy part, you flare during the acts of gathering information and gaining perspective. Prototyping may start with flaring, but then you'll need to focus in order to create the object that will be tested. Knowing if you are focusing or flaring, and respecting where you are—not flaring when you're supposed to be focusing or vice versa—is critical to a successful process (and helpful in not driving your collaborators crazy).

Radical Collaboration

Lastly, design thinking recognizes the power of bringing together lots of different humans with different experiences and backgrounds, to meld as many different inspirations and possible ideas and reach the best possible place.

DESIGN PRINCIPLES

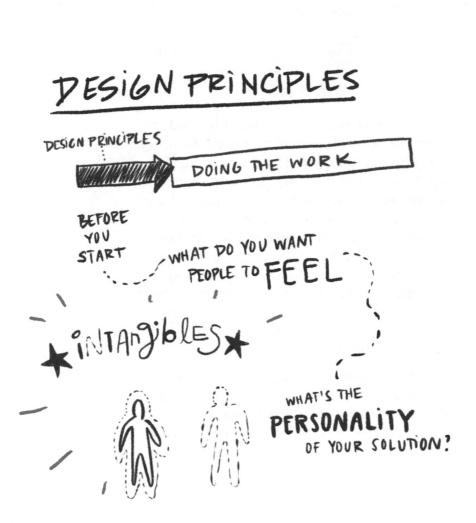

DESIGN PRINCIPLES →→→→ DOING THE WORK

BEFORE YOU START

WHAT DO YOU WANT PEOPLE TO FEEL

★ intangibles ★

WHAT'S THE PERSONALITY OF YOUR SOLUTION?

Design Principles

One of our favorite tools for collaborative design is the use of design principles. Establishing these at the outset of your process is especially helpful if you are trying to create a different experience than the existing culture in which you work. Culture is sneaky; it infuses everything and often shows up in unexpected ways as our work unfolds. It helps to take the time up front, before you start, to talk about how you want people to experience the thing you ultimately create. The key is that you are describing the feelings people have when interacting with your thing, not the thing itself. You are trying to capture the intangibles—essentially the personality of what you will later create.

As we discussed in the last chapter, there are many layers of negative culture surrounding substitute teaching. We see them show up in our work in unexpected ways, like when HR teams slip into calling subs "bodies," or when teachers casually mention that they give subs a stack of worksheets to do with their class because they can't trust them to do anything else. Sometimes, when you are in the thick of trying to figure out what works, you can feel the undertow of the dominant culture. Our design principles remind us to keep focused on the human experience—how people interact with the things we create.

Here are our design principles at Substantial—we are sharing them to give you a tangible example of how you might use this technique in your work:

- **Growth Mindset:** Believe in people and their capacity to change and improve, invite people to see that they can intentionally build their skills.
- **Personal/Human:** Make people feel seen and believed in. Be authentic, approachable, real.
- **Clean Design:** Make people feel cared for through good design and clear writing. Lean toward visuals, go lighter on writing.
- **Playful and Approachable:** There's just a little bit of fun in everything, a sense of energy and optimism. Don't take ourselves too seriously.
- **Empowering:** Set a tone of co-ownership and co-design. Don't position ourselves as "experts" with answers. Raise the bar, and the sense of what is possible.
- **Practical:** Make it useful and relevant. Rooted in the imperfect and messy world of schools, it doesn't need to depend on perfect conditions.
- **Self-Aware:** Endeavor to be conscious of our own biases and blindspots.

We've included directions for creating your own design principles in the Design Moves Playbook found in the Resources chapter.

STEPS TO DEVELOPING AN IDEA

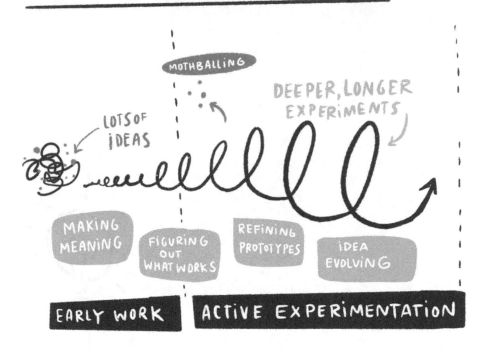

Substantial Classrooms: Redesigning the Substitute Teaching Experience

SOLUTION!

SLOWER, LONGER CYCLES

USABLE THING, BUILT TO LAST!

READY TO USE

Developing an Idea: Steps along the Way

Our goal is to create things that change what happens when teachers are out of the classroom. We'd never have guessed that we'd make an edtech product like SubPlans—but we are clear that the purpose of our design work is ultimately to create already-tested things that we know work. This is why we focus on advancing ideas through the design process toward a product that's ready to be used by lots of people in lots of places. For us, we think of these things as having "graduated" from our Design Lab.

We've noticed that a lot of design thinking resources focus on the early stages of developing an idea, so we wanted to be sure to share with you what we've learned about advancing ideas through multiple cycles. The basic cycle doesn't change; it's still fundamentally moving through the steps of "empathy–insight–make–test," but distinct differences become apparent as you move through the iterations.

Early Work

When you kick off a new project, the early stages of the cycle—empathy and insight—have more formality. We always start with formal interviews, shadowing, and other more structured forms of observation. We also spend time bringing to the surface our own assumptions: if you are trying to get to a fresh way of looking at a problem, it helps to first explore your current understanding of it. It's very natural that you jump to a solution rather than being open to learning through your design work. It's also true that we understand the world through the lens of our own experience. In addition to reflecting on your assumptions going into the process, it's also helpful to reflect on who we are, how that influences how we experience the world, and how it may influence the people we interview.

As we've said, designers are quick to take action and, rather than wondering if an idea will work, they test it. In the earliest phase, you should be testing multiple ideas and learning from all of them.

We like to imagine the design process as a funnel, with lots of early experiments and then a gradual narrowing as you home in on ideas that show potential. A pattern emerges as you refine the ideas through iteration: quick cycles of trying an idea with real people, reflecting on what you learned, making changes, and then trying again. The key is to keep these cycles tight, not investing too much time before you turn to testing.

Early design work also requires being ruthless as you learn: be willing to move on from an idea. Like most people, we tend to fall in love with our ideas and it can be hard to let them go when they don't show promise. One thing that's really helped us is to think about this as "mothballing" ideas. We aren't killing an idea forever; we are just setting it aside for now so that we can focus on ideas with more momentum. We often find ourselves going back to mothballed ideas, either because we think they might work in a new context or because we've discovered a new insight and want to try another iteration.

Creating early prototypes is messy and hands on. Early prototypes should be just enough to get the idea out of your head and into a form with which someone can interact. Our earliest prototypes are often hand-drawn: we sketch out a tool, a web page, or a process. Technology makes it easy to create working prototypes quickly, and our next step is often to create a mock-up using Google forms, Google sites, or a video created on a low-cost platform like Adobe

Spark. At some point, we realize that we've narrowed in on an idea with momentum, and can feel the shift to active experimentation.

Active Experimentation

Active experimentation feels distinct from early work because you are working more deeply on the ideas that showed potential in early prototyping. In this phase, we make them more and more real, digging deeper toward understanding how this thing actually works.

Early prototypes are likely more conceptual—just enough to get the idea out of your head and into a form that someone could interact with in a simulated environment. In active experimentation, we shift to creating functional prototypes that can be tested in real settings, as part of someone's real work life. This adds a layer of complexity: it requires considering how this working prototype interacts with existing processes and systems.

As you move through this phase, your idea usually evolves significantly. With each iteration, you are getting closer to something that can be implemented at scale, so your experiments become deeper and longer. Your most important learning comes from seeing the results and observing people as they interact with your prototype.

We tend to lean away from formal interviews in this phase. We find we glean the richest learning from observation and casual conversation. For example, we've noticed that principals are often late for meetings, so we try to show up early and chat with the office staff while we wait. We often learn more from this informal time than we do from the ensuing conversation with the principal. Office managers and secretaries are the heart of any school and they have the most direct involvement with subs, but they don't often do formal meetings, so sit-down interviews can be awkward. Another strategy we use is to offer office hours or some form of drop-in support. This gives us an excuse to hang out at the school, creating more opportunities for casual conversation.

By this phase you probably have a pretty good grasp on the logistics of whatever it is that you are creating, and need to focus on learning. We try to pay attention to the things that surprise us. When we come upon one of these moments, we ask others about the particular dynamics around it. When we feel ourselves starting to wrestle with what we are hearing, or feel frustrated with what people are telling us, it's a good sign that we are learning something important. Try to force yourself to step back and reflect, rather than correcting the folks testing your idea or doubling down on writing lots of compensating instructions.

Sometimes what you are learning is going to point you in a new direction, like when we struck out on school-based sub recruiting, which led to the realization that having solid plans in place to make subs feel welcome was a deeper need. In retrospect, this seems obvious, but at the time it felt like we kept hitting dead ends. These are moments when you can step back, and tap into whatever reflection method works best for you and your team.

At some moment during this reflection (usually when things seem stuck) an idea will spark. Run with it! Test a new version or a spinoff of your idea. It's fine to set aside the original idea and follow a new thread. If you are struggling to muster enthusiasm for an idea, it's likely time to mothball it. Don't worry if it's advanced and you've done several iterations. The reason we experiment is to learn, and you are definitely learning through the process. We've seen that ideas often resurface when new insights and different conditions present a new opportunity to iterate.

Ready to Use

At some point, your iterations become less dramatic and you receive signals that whatever you've created would be useful, as-is, in multiple settings. You've reached what we think of as the "ready to use" phase of bringing an idea to life. We also think of this as when products or services "graduate" from our Design Lab.

The biggest sign is that feeling of reaching simplicity on the other side of complexity. Whatever you've built seems almost blindingly obvious, as you've tested enough to realize what really helps or solves problems, and not what just sounds good on paper. You've ruthlessly mothballed and pruned, and now have a simple, elegant, and effective thing. Your job shifts to focusing on what you need to bring this solution to more people. This usually means building out training supports that allow leaders to introduce the tool, being clear about how it interacts with existing processes and systems, and telling the story of the solution and how it works (a.k.a. marketing). You might also invest in a polished build, like we did for SubPlans.

At this point in the process, your interactions really slow down and stretch out—now your cycle might be an annual one as you balance consistency with needed changes. In our experience, you never stop iterating and things usually need a deep rethink every 3–5 years (if not sooner). As a team, we need to be intentional about this shift. The energy at the beginning of "ready to use" is intensely focused and energetically quite different from the flare of early design or the rapid iteration of "active experimentation." The reason you do all that work is to end up here, with a solution you think will make a difference. This phase is all about the discipline to go from a prototype to a usable product that is built to last.

SUBPLANS

HOW MIGHT WE GET SUBS TO COME BACK?

MOTHBALLING

SUBPLANS

SUBPLANS ONLINE

SUBPLANS APP

EARLY WORK   **ACTIVE EXPERIMENTATION**

EASY TO USE PLATFORM!

SubPlans

READY TO USE

Journey of an Idea: SubPlans

We wanted to end this chapter with the story of one of our projects to help illustrate what our design work looks like. SubPlans was the first "thing" to graduate from our Design Lab. It's an online platform to help schools prepare for substitute teachers. We like to say it's sub prep made easy. While the final product is so simple and intuitive that the most common feedback we hear is, "I can't believe this doesn't already exist," the process for getting there was messy, iterative, and full of moments of discomfort as we wrestled with what we were learning. You'll notice that we included much of what we learned developing SubPlans in the chapter Start Where You Are.

Early Work

SubPlans came out of our work with schools who struggle to attract and retain enough substitute teachers—schools with less than 50% coverage. Our initial question was "How might we get more subs to go to these schools?" Early prototypes included things like a recruitment flyer to post in local restaurants and a video highlighting the school that we shared on social media. All of our early prototypes belly flopped. Not a single person responded.

But our early work led us to a key insight: the schools we worked with had many subs who came once and never came back. We reframed the question: "How might we get subs to come back?" Interviews with subs provided us with many different avenues to pursue. But one clear theme emerged: subs weren't getting the information they needed, and felt frustrated when they couldn't get help during the day. We also observed that the morning tended to be chaotic, and subs were asking questions of the school secretary during the busiest times. Of all of the things we prototyped for recruitment initially, the only one that seemed to make a difference was having teachers add a note to their sub requests that said where to find the plans for the day.

Active Experimentation

Armed with this new insight, and the glimmer of hope from the mildly successful experiment, we reframed the question again: "How might we get subs better information?" We created a checklist of all the information subs requested: parking information, the bell schedule, a plan for the day. We still cringe when we think about how teachers reacted—it was not good. But, during one uncomfortable meeting, a teacher pulled out the template she had bought from the website *Teachers-Pay-Teachers*. Inspired by this example, we created a template, too. Once again, this fell flat, as not a single teacher used it.

Nonetheless, spending all of this time around teachers and office staff helped us develop more empathy and a deeper understanding of what motivated them. One day, the office manager explained that it made sense that teachers didn't always create robust plans. After all, she pointed out, over half the time no one used the plans so it didn't seem worth the effort. We also noticed that she was the one who was scrambling in the morning, trying to find plans or cobble something together when there were no plans. All of this observation and interaction gave us the idea to bring the process online. This way, we could ensure plans got into the hands of the office managers, and we could use technology to make it easier for teachers to create plans.

We created a working prototype using Google sites and tested it with a friendly teacher. Next, we took it to a conference, where we showed it to dozens of teachers, technology leaders, and principals. The feedback was all about minor tweaks, and several people asked if they could use the tool in their school. This gave us the confidence to move to a full-year test, stretching out the design cycle and testing in a real setting. One of our early partner schools agreed to use the working prototype for an entire school year. It's hard to overstate how much we learned from this period.

Ready to Use

The longer test proved to us that the tool had the potential to make sub prep easier for teachers, which increased the likelihood that they would provide subs with complete plans, and that the plans would be more consistent from classroom to classroom. Making the plans more visible to the rest of the school team also enabled the back-end sharing of resources, and created a new motivation for teachers to make sure their plans were complete. We also saw that the tool was beginning to change the dynamics when new subs arrived. It wasn't perfect, but the school wanted to keep using it.

As a result of our pilot year, we decided to invest in building an app—a big step for a small nonprofit like us. The pressure was on to distill what we had learned in this deeper, longer experiment. Some things were easy: we knew the classroom info section needed more scaffolding so that teachers didn't get bogged down. But other things were harder, like facing the fact that one of our favorite parts of the working prototype—bringing plans online and giving subs Chromebooks when they arrived—wasn't actually working. Filled with doubt, we wondered if maybe the tool didn't work after all.

But the longer we sat with it, the more it became clear that what people valued wasn't bringing subs online—it was the strong template, and efficiencies in planning. We changed the design to prepare print-ready PDFs that office managers print in the morning.

From there, things clicked. After months of wrestling with learning, designing, and overengineering, we had found simplicity on the other side of complexity. SubPlans is a very simple tool. As we've mentioned, the thing we hear most often the first time we show it to educators is, "I can't believe this doesn't already exist." And then, once they've been using it, we usually hear some version of, "It's so easy to use."

Sometimes we feel self-conscious holding up a simple meet-them-where-they-are tool like SubPlans as an example of innovation (and we've learned to ignore the scorn of other edtech humans), but the experience reaffirms our commitment to using design thinking. We have learned so much by watching people use the tool in a real setting. It is the first thing we've made that people actually want, and it is a solid reminder that the best designs come from listening deeply to people, as opposed to focusing exclusively on high level strategy. It's humbling. And exciting.

Takeaways

1. **Find Inspiration in Real People:** The magic of design thinking is starting with interviews and shadowing to understand how people currently experience the world and begin to understand their authentic needs. While we balance this with some statistics, we find that the stories of individual people are what fuel us and sharing those stories is the most effective way to get people to suspend disbelief that substitute teaching could work better.

2. **Think Hack:** What can you do today to learn about the potential impact of your idea? This has become a mantra for our team. It's amazing to see how much you learn by trying something in the real world instead of just talking about it. There is so much quiet resignation in the world of substitute teaching and disbelief that it's possible for it to work better. The best way to counteract this is to try something—it creates momentum like nothing else.

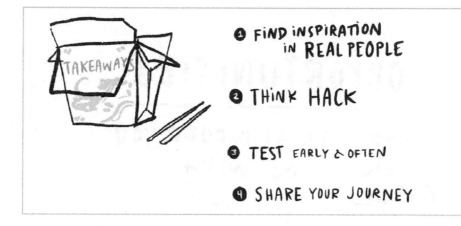

1. **FIND INSPIRATION IN REAL PEOPLE**
2. **THINK HACK**
3. **TEST EARLY & OFTEN**
4. **SHARE YOUR JOURNEY**

3. **Test—Early and Often—in the Real World:** Nothing drives your learning like seeing someone interact with your idea. Rather than describing it, show it and see what happens. As you work iteratively, early prototypes should be rough, but over time they become more complex and fully formed.

4. **Share Your Journey:** Let people know what you are trying to do. Share the stories of subs that inspire you. There is a strong negative narrative around substitute teaching; part of how you create the possibility of something else is to humanize the experience of substitute teaching all around.

Opportunities

We hope that you've emerged from our Design Lab ready to do some design work yourself. In this chapter, we'll introduce six big ideas that we find inspiring in the hope that one will resonate with you. We'll also introduce you to people who are innovating within the substitute teaching systems. Their work inspires us; and we hope it will inspire you, too.

The Heart of the Opportunity: Under-utilized Student Time

We use the term "opportunity" on purpose in this chapter. We believe that the time students spend with substitute teachers is under-utilized and represents a meaningful opportunity to improve the student experience. That's a rare find in our sector—available student time. To make the opportunity even more attractive, it comes with a little bit of funding.

An interesting way to reframe the question of improving substitute teaching is to blow the whole thing up:

What could you do with 10% of student time and $60–250 a day?

While we've highlighted examples of innovators working directly on substitute teaching, we've also come across some intriguing examples of policy entrepreneurs who've identified substitute time as a building block for working on other goals.

We'll start with one example, to show you what we mean. Karen DeMoss is the executive director of Prepared To Teach, a division of the Bank Street Education Center. Karen is on a mission to ensure that aspiring teachers have access to high-quality teacher prep programs. A key barrier for many aspiring teachers is the cost of preparation programs. In addition to the direct program costs, like tuition and the cost of living, the lost income that happens as a result of the time required for completing the field placements can make a teacher prep program out of reach for many of the most desirable candidates.

To address this, Karen and her team set out to find creative ways to fund paid field placements for aspiring teachers. Among the many possible funding sources they identified were those used for substitute teachers. If aspiring teachers spend a day or two a week serving as substitute teachers as an intentional part of their program, while receiving the mentoring and support emerging teachers need, districts can use that funding to help offset the cost of paid field work. While this has the happy side effect of improving coverage for absent teachers, her goal is explicitly focused on preparing new teachers. This is a great example of a policy entrepreneur looking at the substitute teaching challenge both as an opportunity to address other priorities, and as a building block for designing new programs.

Why These Ideas

We've included the following innovations and innovators because one of the fundamental things we learned at the d.school was that simple hacks build the muscles that lead to even greater experimentation. We want you to have some concrete places to start. Additionally, we find that while constraints can seem onerous at first blush, a narrower focus can, in fact, help inspire creativity and minimize the time-suck that deciding/choosing can become. We've done some of the initial synthesis work on these ideas, so your engagement with them can move directly into experimentation.

The ideas included in this section represent a range of approaches, but are by no means exhaustive. Our hope is that you find one (or more!) here that captures your imagination, and you just can't not do it.

Meet the Innovators

The stories we have gathered here for you are about humans who have been working on innovations that relate to substitute teaching. They come from a variety of different roles within the sector, reflecting the simple fact that innovation can come from almost anywhere (and frequently comes from where you'd least expect). They also have a number of things in common, including a solid commitment to the student experience, and the willingness to bring a high degree of flexibility and creativity to the challenge. While interviewing them, we also heard time and time again that the process of being involved with these innovations had changed them personally. They described a degree of hopefulness and resilience that is, frankly, not so present in other discussions we have about substitute teaching. Given that we are only interviewing these people after the fact, it's hard to know which came first, the chicken or the egg: the optimism or the innovation? We're relying on you to give it a try, and then let us know.

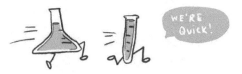

The Art of the Hack

We hope to inspire you to start working on substitute teaching in your context. When you do, we recommend that you start small, think hack. As we've mentioned, the hack is essentially a small, scrappy experiment. It's intended to be low-stakes enough to encourage you to start where you are, to start small and to get moving so that you can build some momentum. A hack is something you can create and try quickly—like, in an afternoon. The idea of a hack is that it's intentionally imperfect, to invite healthy critique and improvement, and so you don't become attached to it. But it is real, and you do engage with others, so it creates mind-blowing opportunities to learn.

Go Forth and Innovate!

Remember, the key to getting started is getting started. So focus on hacks—small changes you can make today that build toward a bigger goal.

Finally, when you do start working—in a small or big way—on reimagining substitute teaching, let us know! We'd love to include you on our list of innovators and connect you with other innovators working in a similar space.

OPPORTUNITY:

Reimagine Substitute Teaching as a Full-Time Fellowship

Substitute teaching is the original gig job—flexible, at-will, day-to-day, and full of uncertainty. What if you turned this on its head and reimagined substitute teaching as a full-time job? Many people come to substitute teaching during times of transition, trying to figure out what to do next. What if you leaned into this and designed a year-long fellowship meant to be a stepping stone to whatever's next?

That's just what the Central Falls School District did. Faced with low coverage and a desire to offer teachers more professional development, they reimagined substitute teaching as a fellowship and transformed how substitute teaching works in their district. What might this look like within your context? We are excited to share this compelling example with you and get you dreaming about the possibilities.

Jay Midwood

Jay Midwood had worked nationally on small learning community grants and secondary school redesign before becoming director of strategy and development for the Central Falls School District in Central Falls, Rhode Island. In some ways, it was an unlikely move. Central Falls is small and has significant challenges: it is the poorest city in the state of Rhode Island, with a median family income of $31,000. But Rhode Island was also home, so making a difference by applying what he'd been working on and learning about felt like the right thing to do.

Jay's involvement with subs was somewhat improbable as well. The way Jay tells the story, he was standing in his living room when he received a call from Victor Capellan, the then superintendent of Central Falls. "Jay," he said, "we need to do something about substitute teaching." The superintendent was convinced that substitute teaching represented an opportunity that could spark local residents with Bachelor's Degrees to become active members of the school community. It was about building economic development and ending poverty by providing credentialed fellows with a well-paying job and a pathway into the field of education. He wanted Jay to figure out how they might flip the script.

So Jay set about writing a new kind of substitute job description. He imagined a fellowship in which the school district committed to 185 days: 180 for teaching and 5 days for PD; one school building so that people could build relationships; and $130/day, raising the rate a little bit, but not too much (Central Falls also offers the option of health insurance and $100/day for these fellows, but most opt for the $130). The teaching fellows program was born.

In the first year, Central Falls received 85 applications for 15 slots. They are now working with their fourth cohort, have 22 available slots, and out of the growing number of applicants, half are from local schools of education. Of the participants, 82% supplement their income by working in after-school and/or summer programs, ultimately building their skills and their connections in the community. And, to date, half end up finding full-time teaching positions after completing the program. For Jay it is both rewarding and bittersweet that his fellows are poached by other districts who identify them as excellent teaching candidates. And Central Falls principals have started coming to Jay for referrals for teacher openings.

Looking back over the past 4 years, Jay says that while the first few years required a well-positioned champion and air traffic controller, the program now has sufficient momentum, and has been successful enough, to have inspired widespread investment in its continuation. Jay has also been thoughtful about the internal district partners he has engaged along the way—from folks in HR to the superintendent, the after-school program director, and the finance director. Jay has built a community of learners working collectively on behalf of the students of Central Falls.

Feeling Inspired?

So are we! It's common for school districts to have full-time subs in their hardest to staff schools but few places have put the level of intentional design into their program that Central Falls has. We hope it inspires you to think about transforming how substitute teaching works in your district.

If you are thinking about experimenting with an idea like this, here are a few tips:

- **Needs a Sponsor:** One thing that makes this fellowship different than other full-time sub programs is the senior level sponsorship. Jay has the authority to not only say how fellows should be used and what support they should receive, but to reinforce those expectations when things don't go as planned.
- **Also Needs a Manager:** In talking with current and former fellows, it's clear that Jay has also stepped into the missing manager role. Fellows talked at length about how important it was to know that Jay was just a call or text away and would always have their backs. He has become an important professional mentor to each fellow, and a key part of their journey.
- **Importance of Teams:** One of the things that makes this program powerful is the placement of fellows in cohort groups. By placing the participants in teams, Central Falls can cover most absences at a particular school while also doing things like releasing teachers for grade-level collaboration. Most fellows have also found mentor teachers on campus who have taught them the ropes, but the day-to-day relationship with their peers is where they have found—and built—community.
- **Time Limited:** Although some fellows continue to a second year, part of what makes this feel different than other full-time sub jobs is that it's designed as a 1-year experience that a cohort engages in together. Creating a decision point at the end of each year also helps to make sure that fellows are there because they want to be, not by default.

OPPORTUNITY:

Part-Time Jobs for College Students

College students need jobs and schools need subs. What if we connected the dots and recruited for substitute teachers on college campuses? Today's college students need to work and are looking for jobs that are part time, flexible, and fit with their academic schedule. That means that they usually end up working in retail, customer service, or restaurant jobs. What if instead we had them working in our classrooms, giving K-12 students a living, breathing example of what it looks like to go to college?

That's just what we experimented with, first with a peer-led cohort at UC Berkeley and later with a one-unit course at Mills College. We found that subbing satisfies college students' desire to stay connected to community and to do work that has a positive social impact. College-age students gave the younger students a dynamic (and usually quite earnest) example of a responsible young adult who has pursued higher ed, is thinking

about careers, and has a broader perspective on the world. It also gave the participating college students a chance to develop career skills like adaptability, communication, and networking. When their subbing was paired with a course, workshop, or other opportunity, the experience afforded them the chance to make meaning and hear advice from both peers and group leaders.

While this idea doesn't work everywhere, it's compelling for districts in states where you don't need a BA, and there are nearby universities. Even if your state requires a BA, it's worth digging around to see if there is an exemption for college students. We did our experiments in California, one of the states that requires a BA but has a special permit available for current college students with 90+ units (this usually means seniors or ambitious juniors).

Celeste Huizar

Celeste Huizar was a UC Berkeley senior when Dave Stark, the executive director at Cal's Stiles Hall, asked if she would be interested in participating in a project that recruited college students to be substitute teachers. Celeste had considered teaching as a possible career after college, and was interested in the opportunity to be in a classroom before committing to a teacher training program or a teaching job, so she said yes. (Full disclosure: this project was sponsored by Substantial.)

Celeste describes the next year as an ongoing learning process. The first challenge was learning how to recruit student participants. She sought out students who would be excited about serving the community that we had initially targeted, were interested in learning, and were committed to mutual support—being relied upon by the other members of the cohort. They also needed to have flexible schedules that would enable them to dedicate 2 days each week to subbing. The group got underway that fall with eight members.

The next phase focused on making sure the participants had the coaching they needed to be successful. The group met weekly, with guest speakers coordinating conversations around classroom management strategies and other education-related topics. Meanwhile, Celeste, again with support, worked with the students to help them obtain permits and identify classrooms. The permitting process proved a significant challenge, and few of the students actually made it into the classroom before the spring.

From Celeste's perspective as a teacher today, she can now see how making the process challenging is important because you want good and committed people, but she also sees the tremendous need for subs, and the pressure it puts upon the system when they aren't available. Also, she notes in looking back on the experience, that an important missing piece was a strong partnership with the district. A district more actively invested in the process might have been able to exert greater influence in the credentialing process, enabling students to move more quickly into the classroom.

Nevertheless, she believes the experience had a positive influence on the participants: two of the eight went on to become teachers. Celeste recalls clearly one conversation that occurred between nervous participants who had not yet begun going into the classroom and those who had. The experienced group shared that despite being quite nervous themselves, they had had an amazing experience. Everyone at the school had been incredibly welcoming, letting them know that they were seen and appreciated, and that their work was valued—they were making a difference.

When Celeste took a year after college to work as an intern in Washington, DC, she couldn't stop thinking about the direct impact she felt like she'd had while teaching. She realized she wanted to be in the classroom. Celeste joined Teach for America the following year, and has been teaching ever since.

Feeling Inspired?

Us too! We continue to be inspired by this practical idea. We've made a guide called *Empowering College Students as Substitute Teachers* that you can find on our website (see information in the Resources chapter).

Here are a few tips if you want to experiment with the idea in your own community:

- **Convener Needed:** A networked convener—be that an individual, a division or administrator from a college, or school district or district leader—provides the structure needed for the students to succeed. It doesn't need to be someone with formal authority, it can be peer-led.
- **Help with Application Process and Costs:** The application process can be complicated and expensive. Assistance in navigating these hurdles dramatically changes the experience and enables students to focus on the more substantive demands of substitute teaching.
- **Anticipate Hesitation from Professors:** Ed school professors are sometimes hesitant about students forming "bad habits" (due to lack of support) or deciding that teaching isn't for them because of negative subbing experiences. This is why we encourage universities to embed substitute teaching in a learning experience. It gives college students an opportunity to build skills that are important to any career, like adaptability, perseverance, the ability to introduce themselves to a group, and the ability to give directions, and gives them a chance to make sense of their experiences.
- **Anticipate Hesitation from District Leaders:** District leaders and principals also have reservations, generally focused on a concern that the age of college students equates to an inability to command the classroom. It can be helpful to point out that college students often have recent experience working with groups of kids in after-school or summer camp settings, and can bring a dynamic, earnest energy to the classroom that translates to a powerful presence.

Community Talent

Substitute teachers are usually asked to continue the regular curriculum, but teachers are quick to tell you they don't expect learning to happen while they are away. What if you embraced this reality and used this time to bring new experiences to your students? Your community is full of creative, compelling people, many of whom have woven together nontraditional careers that give them the flexibility to pursue their passions. What if we reimagined substitute teaching as an opportunity for community members to share their expertise with students?

That's the underlying idea of Parachute Teachers, a different kind of outsourcing firm that matches community members who've developed their own lessons on everything from beekeeping to robotics, with classroom teachers who want to bring those experiences to their students.

Dr. Sarah Cherry Rice

Dr. Sarah Cherry Rice started her career in education as a middle-school teacher in Philadelphia. Her experiences in the classroom were so influential that rather than pursue a career tied to her undergraduate degrees, she decided to remain in education. While conducting a professional development session for math teachers, she found herself in a classroom where no teacher was present. Upon further inspection, she realized there was indeed a sub in the room—at the back, texting, with his feet up on a table.

Sarah came away from the experience curious about the state of substitute teaching. She Googled it and found, as she puts it, that "the headlines were alarming." From a story about a sub who was caught drinking in the classroom, to a tweet of celebratory GIFs showing students leaving school once they realized there would be a sub in the classroom for the day, Sarah was coming to see the issue as far bigger than she had originally understood.

As she continued to research, Sarah realized just how much money and time was being lost when students had a substitute teacher. With the dire shortage of substitute teachers, she also came to understand that many schools spent all morning scrambling to fill classrooms. In response, Sarah began exploring a range of solutions that might allow learning to occur in the classroom even if the main teacher was out for the day.

Believing that community should be a part of schools, Sarah started by examining the assets around a given school, which she quickly identified as being rich with talent. There were chefs, yoga instructors, artists, architects, and even a film producer, all within blocks of her first pilot school. As she interviewed these community members, she heard a recurring theme in their stories—they were excited to share their passions and talents with the next generation.

While on the surface the solution seemed simple and plausible, Sarah had a lot of questions about how she might match local community talent with the needs of schools. Would community members have flexible schedules that would make it possible? Would traditional, risk-averse schools want to try a more innovative solution? How might they change the narrative around "substitutes," which had for decades conjured endless worksheets or the rolling out of a technology cart to watch yet another viewing of the Lion King?

To test this initial idea, Sarah launched a simple website and created a flyer, inviting people to get in touch if they had expertise to share in the classroom. In the first week, over 500 people responded with interests ranging from Egyptian archeology to robotics.

But the question remained: would the schools want these community members to come into their classrooms? To Sarah's dismay, the schools did not initially respond

with enthusiasm. The idea of offering a hands-on learning experience for students overwhelmed schools, who were more focused on the immediate demands of coverage. Nonetheless, managing the sub challenge was a high priority for many, and she was able to identify a few principals who were willing to test her idea. In the beginning, there were some early wins, including one of the first guest instructors: a retired veteran who lived across the street from one of the schools who would roll his mobile ceramics kiln over to the school to teach pottery classes. The students were elated, and anxiously waited each week for him to return.

In the age of online dating, Sarah initially thought of her work as a matchmaking service for schools, replacing the rolodex on the secretary's desk with a modern tool that would seamlessly connect schools with the untapped talent right around the corner in their community. Ultimately, Sarah wanted to expose students to subjects and experts that might not receive as much time or emphasis in the age of standardized testing. For example, the engineer who would parachute in with his 3D printers or the urban farmer who brought farm to table cooking classes to schools located in food deserts.

To begin to scale this model, Sarah launched Parachute, a company supporting districts in integrating community talent into their schools in flexible ways that foster more innovative, hands-on learning. They developed a manual for guest instructors, highlighting basic "teacher moves" such as attention-getters, proximity (actually standing near the student), starting out lessons by sharing a personal story, respectfully navigating someone else's classroom, and ways to effectively use supplies. By creating opportunities for "parachuters" to collaborate, they were better able to create a sense of meaning, mastery, and community. "We had initially thought that we were an edtech company," Sarah explains, "but we came to see that what we're really doing is empowering communities."

Feeling Inspired?

You aren't the only one! Sarah has been profiled dozens of times because her idea is so compelling. We hope it will inspire you to experiment with this in your community. A few tips if you do:

- **Keep Teachers in the Loop:** To make this work, teachers need to prepare their students for a different type of substitute teaching experience, and they need to know that the regular curriculum won't be taught that day.
- **Teachers and Community Members Need to Find Each Other:** Sarah created an outsourcing company because it was the easiest way to create a marketplace for community members to describe their expertise. That's not the only way to do it, but it is important to figure out how teachers and community members will find each other. Start simple, such as a Google site or a meetup.
- **Expertise Doesn't Equal Teaching:** Nonteachers will need some help developing engaging lessons and structuring a day. As Sarah pointed out, awareness of basic "teacher moves"—such as attention-getters, proximity, starting out lessons by sharing a personal story, respectfully navigating someone else's classroom, and methods of effectively using supplies—make a huge difference.

Substantial Classrooms: Redesigning the Substitute Teaching Experience

Teacher Pre-service

Substitute teaching has long been a stepping stone for new teachers, where they gain experience and network to find their first job. What if we designed the experience with this in mind? In our interviews we heard over and over that teacher candidates need to work while they are in school. What if that work was something akin to paid field work— a chance to do applied learning in the real world while you got paid?

John Henning, dean of the School of Education at Monmouth University, is convinced that substitute teaching offers education students a chance to build skills and get ready to step into the classroom. He points out that nearly all of his students need to work and now encourages students to work as substitute teachers in surrounding districts, offering workshops and support to make sure it's also a learning opportunity for his students.

John Henning

John Henning was introduced to the idea of paid internships for student teachers by Karen DeMoss at the Bank Street Education Center (whom we mentioned earlier); and his first reaction was skepticism. He eventually shifted his thinking, deciding that while he still doubted it was actually doable, it seemed like the right thing to do, and was worth a try.

In New Jersey, the requirement for becoming a sub is 60 college credits, so a junior in college could be eligible. As John started poking around, he was surprised to find that there were already students in his program who were taking advantage of this opportunity. Furthermore, they were combining subbing with other field experiences, and were proving to be more comfortable in the classroom than their non-subbing classmates as they had more time in schools and with students. This was evidence for John that student teaching candidates develop faster with more classroom time.

Monmouth already had a year-long field experience program and John began exploring ways to add subbing experiences to extend their engagement. This was easiest for graduate students as they had greater scheduling flexibility. Unique opportunities arose: a district in need of a long-term Spanish class sub had been unable to find someone qualified to teach Spanish. They were willing to create a long-term sub role 3 days a week, and a bilingual undergraduate was able to step in.

To prepare students for subbing, Monmouth now offers a substitute teaching academy in the late summer before school starts. John had started his own teaching career as a sub and was adamant that the key was to prepare them for the worst. He describes the reflections of one of his students, who arrived at a subbing assignment to find no lesson plan or instructions of any kind. John said that he knew Monmouth had succeeded in preparing her when he heard that her response had been, "No one has time to deal with me panicking."

John has thought a lot about how the subbing experience differs from the more traditional student teaching experience. While student teaching emphasizes content delivery, subbing represents a singular opportunity to focus on the skills of relationship building and classroom management. Learning to be a great teacher, John insists, is an iterative process—you come across a challenge, try something, and then reflect and ask for help so you are better prepared the next time. Subbing speeds up this cycle, and provides student teachers with invaluable classroom experience. He has also been happy to see that teachers are enthusiastic about mentoring student teachers over the course of a year, especially when they develop an ongoing relationship with students who can then be reliable and skilled subs.

Feeling Inspired?

We are too! We've seen several examples of colleges and universities beginning to experiment with this idea, and hope to see many more. If you want to experiment with it in your community, here's some practical advice:

- **Embed in Learning:** Just like with undergrads, it's important to provide education students with the support they need to make substitute teaching a positive learning experience. That includes space and support to make meaning of their experiences in the classroom.
- **Student Schedules:** To sub, students need at least 1 day of the week free from classes during the day. This takes planning on the part of students and potentially a rethinking of when key classes are offered.
- **Help with Hiring Process:** As we covered in the Part-time Job for College Students opportunity, district hiring processes can be burdensome and slow. College students, who have a lot going on already and need to be working, find it difficult to make time for repeated trips to the district office. We recommend that you reach out to local districts to ask for help in guiding your students through the process.

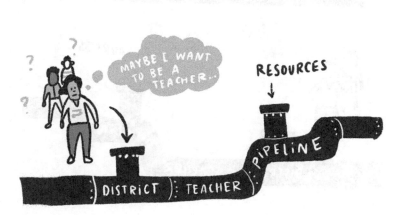

OPPORTUNITY:

District Teacher Pipeline

Substitute teaching has long been a pathway to teaching, where people figure out if teaching is for them and gain early experience. As a sector, we are increasingly focused on the teacher shortage. In our surveys, around 50% of substitute teachers identify as aspiring teachers. What if we reimagined our substitute teaching pool as an intentional new teacher pipeline?

That's just what Fresno Unified has done. The district has created an impressive array of programs to help build their own teacher pipeline. When you talk to the team behind the effort, you realize that they see their substitute teacher pool as a key source of candidates for their pipeline programs. From the moment candidates are interviewed, substitute teachers are invited to apply for the district's pipeline programs and all substitute teachers are supported in developing their skills as teachers throughout their tenure in the district.

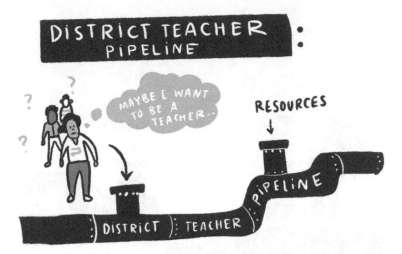

INNOVATOR PROFILE:

Traci Taylor & Jeanna Perry

Fresno Unified School District (FUSD) provides a great counterexample: the district has attempted to address the issue of the missing manager by incorporating the recruitment, interviewing, and ongoing professional development of substitute teachers into their larger teacher development initiatives. FUSD's larger vision is that every classroom will have a highly effective teacher. To this end, they coordinate 18 different initiatives under the umbrella of Professional Learning. Substitute teachers are supported in their own right, and the district has also made an effort to leverage substitute teaching as an opportunity to supplement the income of student teachers during their residencies, encouraging them to sub for their mentor teachers where they have established relationships.

FUSD's unique framing of this approach focuses on finding the "best thing for students." Jeanna Perry, an FUSD Teacher Development staff person, explains that as a district they endeavor to consider every decision from the vantage of how an experience will impact student achievement. When it comes to choosing between having a complete stranger or a resident as a substitute teacher for a classroom, it feels like a pretty obvious choice: the resident knows the students, the teacher for whom they are subbing, and the school and classroom norms.

THE TEACHER POOL!

Unlike in many other districts, substitute teachers are recruited and interviewed by a teacher on special assignment (the original TSA), which creates a stronger connection to instruction for the role. The TSA is responsible for visiting and observing subs, along with others in the teacher development pipeline like student teachers and teaching residents. Subs are also included in broader professional development opportunities, like the district's Saturday seminars on topics including technology, English learning instruction, and special education.

Finally, because subs are included in this broader effort to support teacher development, they have access to alternative pathways to becoming a teacher, like networking with programs including local universities who participate in the district-sponsored Expo. The impact is measurable. Over 40% of the district's new hires—which average between 300 and 400 annually—come from the district's teacher development pipeline. And—in stark contrast with many of the other district staff in charge of subs with whom we've talked—Traci Taylor, another teacher development staffer from FUSD, describes their work as invigorating and transformative, and fundamentally oriented toward supporting the district in providing students with what they need.

Feeling Inspired?

We've seen many districts who've included substitute teachers in their teacher pipeline strategy document, but few who do it as comprehensively as Fresno Unified. We hope it inspired you! If you want to experiment with this in your community, here are a few tips:

- **Start Small:** The staff in Fresno started with 3 very basic programs in their Teacher Development pipeline, and now have 18. Building off their successes has created momentum and excitement around their initiatives that attracts both participants and support from the rest of the district.
- **Include in Sub Recruitment:** Reframing sub recruitment to include teacher development changes the conversation from the outset and serves to signal that it is an aspect of the student experience that you value, and are willing to invest in.
- **Support is Critical:** This strategy backfires if substitute teachers aren't supported, and the experience actually drives them out of teaching.

OPPORTUNITY:

After-School Staff

What if the answer to having more stability in substitute teaching is already on campus? This idea is all about taking a fresh look at existing resources. The key to a positive sub experience for students is relationships and familiarity. This should come as no surprise as the research and best advice about classroom management center on building relationships with students, along with consistency in rules and routines. Current after-school staff have relationships with students, and are often familiar with the school rules and the personalities of different teachers. Most also work second or third jobs during the school day (or evening) to make ends meet. What if we reimagine substitute teaching as a way to meet this need and help after-school staff continue their professional journey?

That's just what Coaching4Change has done, adding substitute teaching as an option for their coaches and providing the support that they need to persist in the job. It's a new service they offer to their partner districts, and it has contributed to their effectiveness and impact as a nonprofit organization.

Marquis Taylor

Marquis Taylor is the co-founder and president of a Massachusetts-based nonprofit organization called Coaching 4Change (C4C). In 2013, the program introduced formalized college mentorships, allowing college students to be volunteer mentors at C4C after-school sites. A few years later, a principal at a C4C school was experiencing a massive shortage in substitute teachers, and asked Marquis if any of the C4C mentors might be interested. While the requirements vary in different districts in Massachusetts, this particular district allowed college students with 60 credits to sub, and though the district's allotted $80/day wasn't a lot, for a college student it was significant.

To start, Marquis agreed to test the idea of recruiting his mentors to become subs at one school. C4C was already absorbing some of the onboarding costs—fingerprints and background checks—and they took on the sub application process as well. During that first year, ten mentors worked after school in the C4C program, four became subs, and two mentors got full-time teaching positions within the district upon graduating from college.

Marquis is quick to point out that there were some bumps that first year, and some important learnings. There had been concerns about transportation, but the mentors were quick to self-organize, creating a buddy system and ride-sharing. Still, the C4C staff could see that focusing on districts within a 30 min driving radius was essential to ensuring that their mentors actually showed up. There was also a lot of learning to be done around setting expectations. Marquis reminded districts that these young people were very newly initiated into the world of adulthood, and a greater degree of clarity

about timeliness, protocols, and procedures was often necessary to set them up for success. In addition, Marquis worked with the districts and school leadership to help them see the C4C mentors as not only substitute teachers, but also a strategic pipeline for a future workforce.

This year the program has expanded to include 35 coaches subbing in 3 different districts. As Marquis sees it, the biggest challenge is in acclimating mentors to the school culture and community. "Plopping in as a short-term sub is just really hard," he offers. "How are you supposed to know that a teacher wants you to have the students put their chairs on top of their desks? And then they can get so mad if you get it wrong!"

Marquis sees C4C as an opportunity for school districts to reimagine after-school time and substitute teaching as a pathway for attracting new talent—in particular, teachers of color. He is convinced that this new aspect of C4C is filling a gap that makes a huge difference, while offering after-school staff something they really need—meaningful, paying part-time work.

Feeling Inspired?

We hope so! Coaching4Change offers program design consulting for other organizations, so they are a good resource if you want to explore their model. If you are going to experiment with this idea, here are some things to keep in mind.

- **Think About the Schedule:** Working as a sub during the school day and then working in an after-school program makes for a very long day. Be creative about how to structure the schedule so that staff who work during the day aren't the same ones who close the after-school program.
- **Eligibility Might be an Issue:** Typically, there are different education requirements for after-school staff and subs. Some may not be eligible to do both.
- **How it Fits into Management:** The good news is that you likely already have a manager in place who supervises and supports your after-school staff. It's exciting to think that you can extend that feeling of support to when they work as subs—to address the "missing manager" problem—but it's added work for them. Think about this as part of program design.

Emerging Opportunities

For most of the opportunities in this chapter we've included concrete examples in the form of *innovator profiles*. We think reading the stories of the people behind the examples is the best way to inspire you to take action. But we also wanted to include a few compelling ideas without concrete examples. That's not to say there aren't any; only that we have yet to find them. Who knows— maybe one of you will create one! If you do, be sure to tell us so we can share your story with others.

Cross-Generational Relationships
Connecting Neighbors to Schools

We were inspired by our friends at the AARP Foundation to think about pre-retirement aged people who are searching for mean- ingful paid employment—think 50–65 year- olds. This is the age when people begin experiencing age discrimination, so falling out of the paid labor market for any reason can make it harder to find your way back in.

There are a number of attributes that make this population partic- ularly compelling. Older adults have had more life experiences to draw on and often possess a quiet authority that comes with age. School leaders are excited about building deeper connections with the community surrounding a school, and this is a concrete way to do it. Some people in this age bracket are looking for second careers, and substitute teaching can be a pathway into the pro- fession. If you are inspired to experiment with this idea, check out the AARP Foundation's Back to Work 50+ program for additional resources.

Student-Directed Learning

This idea comes from the folks at the Teacher's Guild, a self-described "professional community that activates teachers' creativity to solve the biggest challenges in education today." If you aren't familiar with them, we'd recommend you check out their website (https://www.teachersguild.org).

Here's the idea: create an ongoing alternative routine for days when high school students have substitute teachers. Instead of the regular curriculum, students work on their own special project—one that they work on throughout the year, making progress each time they have a sub. Inspired by Google's "20 percent time" (the practice that allows employees to take time out of their regular job to pursue a side project), Charlie Shryock, director of faculty development at Bishop McNamara High School in Forestville, Maryland, came up with the idea. This "substitute teacher hack" creates opportunities for students to direct their learning and spend time on work that sparks their personal interests, making the most of the time when the regular classroom teacher is absent.

Reverse Field Trips

Imagine if you could bring your students a special learning experi-ence while ensuring that your teachers could attend PD. There are many ways that this idea might take shape, but at its root the idea is to flip the idea of the traditional field trip, bringing the experience to the students instead of having the students leave the building. In our early experiments we imagined this as a partnership between a school district and a local organization with an interest in educating students on a specific topic, like a science museum or arts educa-tion program. Our hope was that reverse field trips would happen on pre-planned teacher training days, helping to make sure that kids were learning as much as their teachers on these days (and also triggering the availability of Title II dollars). As a new service they could offer, the reverse field trip represents a potentially new revenue stream for the community organization, enabling them to expand their impact and reach.

Tandem Subbing

One of the big reasons people don't get into subbing is because they're understandably daunted by the idea of finding themselves alone in front of a classroom full of kids with little-to-no training. But what if they didn't have to be alone? What if it was possible to become a sub alongside somebody else? If both people were certified as subs, you could take turns being the teacher of record and alternating who got paid. You could work as a pair until you were comfortable enough to go it alone or, if the money wasn't an issue for you, you could sub as a pair in perpetuity—occasionally switching in rookie subs who appreciated the opportunity to have a shadow day before going it alone. Seriously, if you try this—let us know!

Military Spouses

It turns out many military spouses are already actively working as substitute teachers in many areas across the country; and for districts that are near a base, it's a population worth actively recruiting. We first encountered this phenomenon through a connection to the Fort Campbell army base in Kentucky. For a small community like nearby Clarksville, Tennessee (just across the state line), Fort Campbell is the largest local employer, so it's not particularly surprising that there's someone connected to the base working at just about every school in the Clarksville district. Often spouses new to a military base, especially ones with little children and service member partners who may be deployed at any moment, like the flexibility of working as a sub, especially when they can do it at the schools their children attend. Moreover, the military often has resources that support spouses in offsetting costs related to credentialing.

Takeaways

- **Great Things Are Already Happening.** There are a lot of amazing things already happening to improve the substitute teaching experience. Take inspiration from the work of your colleagues in other places.
- **There are People behind Innovative Ideas.** Change starts with, and depends upon, humans who are willing to run headlong at a challenge.
- **It's not a Linear Path.** Your ideas more than likely won't work out exactly as you initially imagined. Real change is messy and iterative.
- **Look for the Bright Spots.** Find your inspiration from what is working and try to figure out how to make more of it.

CONCLUSION

THE COMMENCEMENT CHAPTER!

The Commencement Chapter

We are suckers for commencement speeches. You take a lifetime of experience and squish it into 15–20 min of insight and wisdom from a famous person, in springtime. Seriously, what could be better? The whole idea behind a commencement speech is brilliant right out of the gate. It's both an acknowledgment that something is coming to an end, and a framing of that ending as a new beginning. You mix in a bit of humor and some tear-jerking inspiration and boom—YouTube gold. So, it feels kind of cheesy and embarrassing to admit that that's what we want for our concluding chapter. We've told you our story and the stories of a whole bunch of other inspiring people—and now we're hoping that you will go out and write your own.

When we first started working on the issue of substitute teaching, one of the things that we heard most was surprise. And the surprise wasn't around the question of substitute teaching being an issue. There was universal agreement that substitute teaching, in its current configuration, really didn't work for anyone involved. The universal surprise was around the fact that seemingly un-crazy humans would elect to spend their time on this issue.

And then, almost just as universally, people at all levels of education—principals, teachers, superintendents, ed school professors—followed up their expression of surprise with the comment, "I actually started teaching as a sub." They'd tell us some sort of story about what they'd learned subbing, or how bad their initial experience had been, and then consistently added that they had been, of course, different than a "regular" sub.

We wanted to ensure that this book was filled with stories, because while the narratives about subs that are prevalent in our popular culture are pretty grim or ridiculous (the aforementioned Key and Peele, *Miss Nelson is Missing*, or that cinematic classic, *The Substitute*), our work has exposed us to all sorts of stories that have left us feeling absolutely convinced that good things are already happening; that there are lots and lots of people out there who don't see themselves as the "regular" sub, and whose stories point toward all sorts of better opportunities for kids.

Using the design lens in this work has many benefits to recommend it, but perhaps the biggest is the introduction of empathy as a magic shortcut to a deeper understanding of an issue. If you take nothing else away from this book, we hope it is this: taking the time to talk with people in the roles you hope to influence is invaluable. And actually shadowing them in their day-to-day borders on mind-blowing.

We knew, as we set about writing this book, that we wanted to share what we were learning about the state of substitute teaching—the sheer magnitude of its influence in schools and the paucity of actual research on the breadth of its impact. We also knew that we wanted to share some practical tips on things that people could do—immediate steps that could be taken to improve the situation—that encouraged you, the reader, to really understand your own context and then to start where you are.

And we really wanted to share our excitement about the process of design as a revelatory and joy-infusing approach to making sense and improving the world around us. Maybe it's because it's all still so new to us, and we're still fueled by the fervor of the neophyte, but we are more than convinced that when given the opportunity to redesign/rethink/think deeply about our work, it helps us to thrive as individuals. The process itself builds community and increases our sense of humanity. Our job—our hope—in writing this book is to inspire you to embrace this redesigning work as your own.

Your own journey of understanding and meeting the challenges of substitute teaching is best served by actually jumping in and doing. Doing leads to learning. When you start with small hacks, our experience is that larger change is likely to follow. By helping individuals thrive, you work indirectly to bolster the system within which you operate through empathy and collaboration. It starts with you.

We hope that you take away a number of different lessons from the innovators that we've highlighted, but most importantly, we hope you come away with the sense that you are not alone. This work is do-able. You now have the design thinking tools and mindsets that make it so. We hope that you'll dig more into the additional resources that we've included here in the Resources chapter, as well as the materials we have on our website. Finally, we hope that you will begin to see the world around you as a boundless opportunity for experimentation, a journey waiting to be taken that will leave you feeling inspired and effective in improving the experience of substitute teaching for everyone.

Thank you.

Resources

We've gathered a few resources that we think will be helpful. You can find more on our website: substantialclassrooms.org.

Design Moves Playbook

While there are numerous guides to design thinking written by far more experienced practitioners (many of which we happily point you to in a few pages), we none-theless wanted to set you up with some introductory, rookie-friendly, handy-dandy design moves that you could play with as you begin to explore the state of substitute teaching in your world.

One observation to start: we have found that the most successful design efforts occur when we go into a process with clear intentions and a solid plan that is focused on making the humans participating feel the most seen and valued, and then being brave enough to let go when things go in a completely different direction than we'd anticipated. It's a little counterintuitive—wedding intentional design to an almost Buddhist commitment to letting go—but it does seem to create the best results and most pleasant experiences. In some ways, it's a lot like parenting. Who knew?

Card Sort

Why—You're going out to interview someone about something you think they might be a little reticent to discuss, and/or haven't really thought about much yet.

How—Think of a question you're interested in asking, and then write out five to seven different possible answers on index cards. Try making some of the answers a bit extreme.

What—Ask the question to the person you're interviewing. Hand them the cards and ask them to sort the cards top to bottom in order of relevance to the question. Take note of how they touch the cards and move them around, what they say to themselves as they move the cards, and especially note when things seem inconsistent—like, they're saying that one card isn't relevant, but they can't seem to take their hand off it.

Example—When Jill first started interviewing principals about substitute teachers, she wrote out the attributes that principals might possibly value in a sub: *punctual, excellent with students, good hygiene, interested in becoming a teacher, flexible*. Jill learned a lot by watching the principals move the cards around and talk themselves through their thoughts about the attributes that mattered most. The cards gave the principals a structure for thinking more deeply about their own practical needs as opposed to answering the question with more theoretical and unconsidered answers.

Shadow Day

Why—Shadow days are distinct from empathy interviews; there are some things that need to be experienced to be fully understood.

How—Ask the person you are interested in better understanding if you could spend a day—or a part of a day—shadowing them.

What—An intentional observation exercise in which one shadows someone, taking notes about the time spent on assorted tasks and the moods and emotions accompanying the different activities.

Example—School Retool's annual *Shadow a Student Challenge* (http://www.shadowastudent.org) invites school principals to spend an entire day shadowing a student in their school to get a more comprehensive perspective on the actual experience of being a student in their school.

Journey Mapping

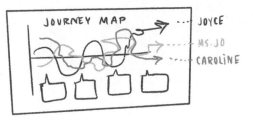

Why—To deepen understanding and inspire empathy for someone's experience.

How—Give them a piece of paper and ask them to draw out a specific experience or time frame. The paper can be marked to promote more of a linear representation of the journey from left to right, with high points and low points. This can also be done in a more free-form way, by providing a blank piece of paper and asking them to draw the journey as they see fit.

What—Once the visual representation of the person's journey is created, the interviewer can ask the creator to walk them through their process. Save questions for after the initial walkthrough, and pay special attention to the creator's comments about things that surprised them, any inconsistencies between what they say and what their visual suggests, and other details that strike you as unexpected. After the person has talked you all the way through, dig into the areas where they seemed most energetic, as well as areas they may have failed to call out.

Example—During Jill's fellowship at the d.school, one of the other fellows, Ashanti, agreed to go into a local school district office and apply to be a sub. When he walked Jill through his journey map of the visit to the office, he had casually mentioned how he'd been surprised by their enthusiasm about his becoming a sub. While Ashanti insisted that it was no big deal, he kept coming back to their reaction. After he had finished describing the interaction, Jill asked if he'd found their reaction troubling in some way, or if he had any more thoughts about it, and Ashanti paused for a moment, "You know," he said, "they wanted me so badly, it made me not want to do it, like, there must be something wrong."

"How Might We" Questions

Why—One of the biggest challenges of design is getting to the right question. As humans, we are very oriented toward solving problems, but sometimes this means that we jump to problem-solving before we've adequately defined the problem.

How—After doing some empathy interviews, set up a description of the person you talked to and their challenge in the form of a Mad Lib:

> We met (*name*), a (*brief description*), who needs to (*their need*) because (*surprising insight*).

What—Once you have the need worked out, play around with alternative ways of framing the problem, all starting with the magic three words: "How Might We" (a.k.a. HMW).

Example—When Amanda first went to work with a group of schools that had very low fill rates, everyone assumed the problem they were trying to solve was: "HMW get more people to sub at our school?" After Amanda had the chance to work with some of the staff and conduct interviews with some of the subs, they were able to reframe the question as: "HMW get our best subs to come more frequently?"

Assumption Storming

Why—When entering into the process of defining a problem and/or making sense of the information we have gathered, it is often useful to call out the assumptions we might be bringing with us into the process so that they are less likely to get in the way of new thinking.

How—Stand near a wall, with everyone armed with a pad of Post-its and a Sharpie. Have people call out, and then write down and post, all the assumptions they have about the issue or question at hand. Participants should be listening to one another's assumptions to spark new ideas, building off what others share.

What—Once people have generated assumptions for 5 min, create a space to discuss these assumptions and ask one another questions about them. One helpful followup activity is to go through all of the assumptions, and then write up an assumption that is the exact opposite of the original assumption.

Example—When we first started working on the substitute teaching question, we hosted a design session at Stanford and invited current teachers and school administrators to share their assumptions about the subs in their schools. They shared everything from "There aren't enough subs" to "The people who want to sub aren't qualified to be teachers." When we flipped these assumptions into affirmative statements—"There are more than enough subs available" and "The people who sub would be great teachers"—it dramatically changed the tone and focus of the conversations that followed.

Design Principles

Why—Articulating values at the outset of your process is especially helpful if you are trying to create an experience that is different from the existing culture in which you work.

How—At the start of your next project, take the time to define your design principles. In our experience, it's helpful to do this over two meetings. It's a quick exercise, maybe 10–20 min. Ask yourself, how do we want people to experience the things we ultimately create? How do we want it to make them feel? Brainstorm it as a group and look for the things that get people most excited. You want these to give you a little "zing!" up your spine. They should make you feel like: "Yes! That is the work I want to put out into the world." Design principles are best if they are expressed in quick, casual language. Resist the urge to put them into overedited formal language (we've all seen those mission statements that were written by a group unwilling to make tradeoffs). That's why it's helpful to do this as a two-step exercise—someone can type them up and then you can revisit them the next meeting to see if you feel that zing. Chances are you will cut a few at that point, and maybe add a few. Once you've got them down, it's great to quickly revisit them (as in, say them out loud) at the beginning of every project team meeting. We also have ours posted on the wall of our workspace.

What—Rather than describing the thing itself, describe the feelings you want people to have when interacting with the thing. You are trying to capture the intangibles—essentially, the personality of what you will later create.

Example—These are Substantial's Design Principles:

- **Growth Mindset:** Believe in people and their capacity to change and improve. Invite people to see that they can intentionally build their skills.
- **Personal/Human:** Make people feel seen and believed in. Authentic, approachable, real.
- **Clean Design:** Make people feel cared for with good design and clear writing. Lean toward visuals, go lighter on writing.
- **Playful and Approachable:** There's just a little bit of fun in everything, a sense of energy and optimism. Don't take ourselves too seriously.
- **Empowering:** Set a tone of co-ownership and co-design. Don't frame ourselves as "experts" with answers. Raise the horizon and sense of what is possible.
- **Practical:** Make it useful and relevant. Rooted in the imperfect and messy world of schools, it doesn't depend on perfect conditions.
- **Self-Aware:** Endeavor to be conscious of our own biases and blindspots.

Brainstorming

Why—When done well, brainstorming can inspire new ways of considering the challenge and help generate innovative solutions.

How—There are lots of different ways to brainstorm, but we like to make sure we have a comfortable space with everyone participating in possession of their own Sharpie and a pad of Post-its—as we described in the Assumption Storming directions above. The four key rules to high-quality brainstorming are: (a) no judgment; (b) all ideas are welcome (this is not the moment to be tripping on reality); (c) quantity over quality (seriously, it is often the idea that comes at the very, very end of a brainstorm that takes the prize); and (d) more humans, with more perspectives, is better. You can brainstorm alone, but getting it out of your own head and engaging with others contributes to higher quality ideas.

What—We're particularly fond of two specific approaches— Constraints and Analogous Situations. In brainstorming with constraints, you approach a challenge with a specific set of conditions—such as "only solutions that cost over $100,000," or "involve magic," or "are the worst possible ideas/illegal," or, our favorite, "involves Dwayne 'The Rock' Johnson." Spending time brainstorming with a number of different constraints can open up greater creativity for more direct brainstorming. Brainstorming with analogous situations is a three-step process. You begin by brainstorming the conditions of the current challenge you're addressing—you're looking for adjectives like "stressful," or "lonely," or "hungry." Then you brainstorm other situations where you find these conditions addressed successfully. The third step is to brainstorm ways that you might make your challenge more like the analogous situation(s) you've identified.

Example—When we were first working on Substantial, we did an analogous brainstorm and determined that being a Forest Firefighter was comparable to being a substitute teacher and, as a result, designed a backpack with the "rescue supplies" that a sub would want to have when dropped into the unstaffed classroom: a joke book, some puzzles, a book of riddles, a ball, some cones, a book of short stories to read aloud, etc. The Sub backpack was the very first iteration of the idea that would ultimately become Sub-Plans! (The other analogous role was Superhero and that is how our logo came to have two lightning bolts—it was either that, or issue a cape to everyone involved with the project.)

Prototyping

Why—A prototype is essentially an early sample of one's idea made real. It can be a sketch or a skit or a craft project; the goal is to convey the core functionality of the idea in question. There are a bunch of whys for prototyping—these make you actually move from the theoretical to the practical, enable you to interact in a different way with your idea, and invite other people in to experience the idea in a tangible way.

How—Prototypes come in basically three speeds—low-fidelity (lo-fi), medium-fidelity (medium-fi), and high-fidelity (high-fi). Lo-fi prototypes are often paper. Medium-fi prototypes reflect a bit more effort and generally have some of the proposed practical functionalities in operation. High-fi prototypes are generally what one uses when going out into the real world to test.

What—Prototypes can come in all shapes and sizes—from something worked up using Google tools, to a pre-recorded video that plays in response to a request for a service online, to a full-blown set designed to simulate the interaction one is hoping to create.

PROTOTYPE & TEST

Example—In our section on the SubPlans app, we describe how we built some of the core functionalities of the app in Google to test it. We spent a year watching how the schools used the prototype to more cost-effectively direct developers in building out the product. One key example of this was that we had initially assumed that subs would want to get the lesson plans online, but quickly came to understand that they wanted the plans printed out, and the school secretaries were the key people making sure that they received the printed plans. This inspired us to incorporate a printtopdf function (something our developers were seriously resistant to) and to make sure that school secretaries had administrative access to all the teachers' plans.

Feedback

Why—Humans are just generally bad at providing feedback that is consistent, concrete, and constructive. Giving and getting feedback are muscles that need to be exercised frequently if one hopes to be good at them.

How—Bake in dedicated time at the end of gatherings where feedback would be useful, like meetings or trainings or workshops, to normalize the process so that there is an expectation that "this is just what we do—good or bad." This helps to avoid having feedback be associated with things going badly.

What—There are a number of variations on the theme of encouraging people to share things they appreciated and things that they'd like to see done differently. You could ask people to share an "I like . . ." an "I wish . . ." and an "I wonder . . .." You could also add Post-its to a 2-by-2 chart that has a heart in one corner, a minus sign in one corner, a question mark in one corner, and a lightbulb in the last corner, and invite comments on things people liked and disliked, or questions that arose and ideas that were generated.

Example—We have added a feedback form to our SubPlans app that creates a structured opportunity for subs to share observations from their day—the good, the bad, and everything in between. For many subs, this invitation to offer feedback is a welcome connection, as opposed to having the only feedback requested of them being via incident reports.

Reflection Tools

Why—People who work in education know that reflection is important
for our students, but we're generally
pretty bad about making it happen
for ourselves. Because people learn
in a myriad of ways, baking it into
the design process is critical to maxi-
mizing the learning that your design
work can generate.

How—Identify a number of different
strategies to prompt reflection and
then formally schedule them, just as you would a meeting.

What—Different reflection tools can include: a quick phone or video
confessional, taking 5 min to free write, pair-share interviews, leaving
a voicemail message that answers two to three reflective questions,
or having a reflective group discussion which is then boiled down
into a haiku or limerick to be shared with the larger group. The
format is really less important than the intentionality of prompting
people to reflect and then giving them a framework to fall back on.

Example—When we did our first sub training at the Stanford
d.school, we distributed small journals. At the end of every section of
the training, we left 5 min for folks to write impressions and observations about the unit they had just experienced. At the end of the
day, we gave people a few minutes to look back over what they'd
written and to share reflections from the day.

Getting Ready
for a Substitute Teacher:
Sample Lesson Plan

Our friends at the Center for Collaborative Classrooms have generously shared this lesson plan from their Caring School Communities Curriculum[1]. We are happy to include it here as a tangible example of classroom practices that make a difference.

ABOUT STUDENT-DIRECTED DECISION MAKING

The class meeting models a process for student-directed decision making in which the students generate ideas and suggestions about how to approach a topic or situation. After this meeting, the students try out their ideas and check in on how things went. You may decide to use this format to address problems or situations in which there are several courses of action (for example, how to welcome visitors to the classroom or what to do when students finish their work early). If possible, plan to have this class meeting just prior to the first substitute teacher's day in your class. You may want to adapt this class meeting to discuss specialty teachers and other adult visitors to the class. This lesson may take more than one class period.

Lesson Purpose:

- Students: discuss and agree on ways to behave responsibly with a substitute teacher.
- Write a letter to a substitute teacher describing how they will act.
- Give reasons for their thinking.

Materials:

- Chart paper and a marker.
- Writing paper and pencils.
- "Class Meeting Rules" chart.

---

1   "Getting Ready for a Substitute Teacher," a component of the Caring School Community® program © 2004. Reproduced with the permission of the publisher.

Substantial Classrooms: Redesigning the Substitute Teaching Experience

The Lesson

1. Gather in a circle and discuss giving reasons for your thinking

Have the students come to the circle with partners sitting together. Briefly review the class meeting rules. Remind the students that they have been working to build a community in their classroom. Explain that today they will talk about how to be responsible and helpful when a class has a substitute teacher. Explain that during today's discussion you would like the students to focus on giving reasons for their thinking whenever they share their ideas. Tell them that you will check in with them at the end of the meeting to see how they did.

2. Generate ideas for behaving responsibly with a substitute teacher

Ask and briefly discuss:

Q: What do you like about having a substitute teacher?

Q: What can be challenging about having a substitute teacher?

Describe what a day with a substitute teacher in their class might be like (or, if you are planning to be out, what will happen on that day). Facilitate a discussion about how the students will take responsibility for themselves at various times during the day. Use "Turn to Your Partner" to discuss:

Q: What are some ways you can welcome the substitute into our community at the beginning of the day?

Q: How can you be responsible when it is time to begin [writer's workshop]?

Q: How can you be helpful when it is time to [go to lunch]?

Q: What are some ways you can be responsible at the end of the day when [you're getting ready to go home]?

For each question, have a few volunteers share their ideas with the class. Record the suggestions on chart paper. Remind the students to give reasons for their thinking as they share.

Students might say:

"I think we can put our name tags out on our desks because that will help the substitute learn our names."

"We can take out our folders and quietly work on our stories. I think that is responsible because then we won't get behind in our writing while you're gone."

"I agree with [Shana], because we should work as hard as we do when you are here."

"In addition to what [Romeo] said, we could show the substitute how we use lunch cards. I think that is helpful because then the substitute won't be confused."

As the students share, ask follow-up questions such as:

Q: Why is it important to try to make the substitute feel welcome in our community?

Q: What questions do you have for [Marla] about her thinking?

Write letters to the substitute teacher

Explain that each student will write a letter telling the substitute how he plans to be responsible and helpful during the day. Review the students' charted ideas and encourage them to include some of these ideas in their letters. Explain that the letter should list at least three things they will do to be responsible or helpful when the class has a substitute teacher. Have the students return to their seats and give them time to write their letters. When they have finished, have several volunteers read their letters aloud to the class. Let them know that all their letters will be bound into a book for substitutes and the class to read during the year. The book will let substitute teachers know that the students have agreed to act in responsible and helpful ways with them. (Note: you may want to write a class letter to the substitute, using the students' brainstormed ideas, rather than having each student write a letter.)

Reflect on the meeting

Remind the students that you expect them to act in the ways they described in their letters and that you will check in with them to see how things went after they have a substitute. Briefly discuss how the students did giving reasons for their thinking during the discussion.

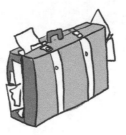

Resource Guide:
Learning About Design Thinking

Organizations

We are active learners and love to participate in events and workshops. These organizations are all great places to learn, and they have robust resources available online:

Stanford's d.school (https://dschool.stanford.edu)
Our favorite place to learn, Stanford's d.school, offers incredible workshops. If you can't make it to Palo Alto, their website is a great place to start. Check out their resources section, which they describe as "a curated collection of resources from our classes and workshops."

School Retool (https://schoolretool.org)
School Retool's primary focus is a fellowship for principals to learn about hacking toward the big ideas from the Deeper Learning framework. We are including them here because we are huge fans of their work, and they have a great website. Be sure to check out their videos introducing the hack mindset.

IDEO.org (https://www.ideo.org)
IDEO.org is a nonprofit design studio. In addition to doing design work, they also create tools that help people learn and practice human-centered design. Their tools are free and easy to access. We loved their online course on Human-Centered Design and have a copy of their Field Guide to Human Centered Design on our desk right now.

Substantial (https://substantialclassrooms.org)
We've also got resources for you on our website. Check out our Design Lab, and find updated stories, tools, and other things you can download and use.

Reading

A curated list of our favorite design books and articles:

Creative Confidence, by Tom and David Kelley

If you read just one book on design, make it this one. Not only will it introduce you to human-centered design, it will make you believe in your own creativity.

Make Space: How to Set the Stage for Creative Collaboration, by Scott Witthoft and Scott Doorley

Visiting the d.school makes you a believer in the powerful role a space can play in driving collaboration and creativity. This book is sure to have you thinking about the design of your meeting rooms and other spaces for collaboration.

Human-Centered, Systems-Minded Design, by Thomas Both, Stanford Social Innovation Review

And while we admit to complete bias, we're big fans of Thomas Both's article in the Stanford Social Innovation Review, "Human-Centered, Systems-Minded Design" because it highlights our work at Substantial while also doing an excellent job of highlighting how both human-centered and systems-thinking methods fit within an effective design approach, and can work in conjunction to address social challenges.

Exposing the Magic of Design, by Jon Kolko

This isn't the book to start with, but it's a great deep dive into synthesis—perhaps the most opaque part of the design process. We loved it.

Additional Reading

The Art of Innovation,
by Tom Kelley

Insight Out,
by Tina Seelig

Change by Design,
by Tim Brown

Weird Ideas That Work,
by Robert Sutton

Wired to Care,
by Dev Patnaik

Rapid Viz,
by Kurt Hanks and Larry Belliston

The Third Teacher: 79 Ways You Can Use Design to Transform Teaching and Learning,
by Cannon Design, VS Furniture, and Bruce Mau Design

Designing Your Life,
by Bill Burnett and Dave Evans

Resource Guide:
Research on Substitute Teaching

At Substantial we keep a running list of the research we've come across that is related to substitute teaching. We've included a curated list here, but it's probably easier to access it on our website, where we link directly to the article, report, or website when possible. *Notice something that's missing? Let us know!*

Start Here—SubNation

Published by *Gatehouse Media*, one of the largest publishers of locally-based print and digital media in the US, this report synthesizes recent research and provides an overview of the challenges related to substitute teaching. It's a great place to start.

General

- **Frontline Institute:** Frontline makes the absence management software most commonly used by both districts and outsource providers. They have a research division that analyzes that data for trends.

- **NCTQ District Trendline:** Substitute Teachers: *District Trendline* provides actionable research to improve district personnel policies that will strengthen the teacher workforce. This September 2017 issue looks at districts' qualifications for their substitutes as well as their compensation.

- **No Substitute for a Teacher:** This news analysis from *Education-Next*, a scholarly journal published by the Hoover Institution, uses a first-person story—the author's son—to personalize the current landscape depicted by research.

  - **Substitute Teachers Are A Large Presence in American Schools:** An accompanying press release from *Education-Next* for "No Substitute for a Teacher."

- **National Education Association:** A Report and Recommendations to Professionalize Substitute Teaching: This downloadable report from the National Education Association makes recommendations to professionalize substitute teaching to draw more qualified individuals into the field.

- **Substitute Teaching Undergoes New Scrutiny:** *Edweek* provides a broad overview of teacher absenteeism data and policy responses in this 2012 article.

- **No Substitute Left Behind:** This article from *Principal* magazine makes a case that school administrators and faculty can improve the substitute teaching experience for all involved by creating positive interactions with the substitute teacher.

- **Status of Substitute Teachers:** A State-By-State Summary: From the National Education Association website, this state-by-state summary gives a snapshot of certification requirements and key issues state-by-state. While it is the most updated list we've found, note that it was compiled back in 2000–2001.
- **1 In 3 Chicago Public Schools Went Without A Teacher For a Year**: NPR story on the teacher shortage, focusing on Chicago Public Schools. Includes an analysis of how sub coverage varies across different schools within the district.

Substitute Teacher Shortage

- **Association of WA (State) School Principals Sub Shortage Survey:** Principals responded to this survey that looked at teacher and substitute shortages, qualifications of candidates, and ability to fill vacancies.
- **Association of WA (State) School Principals Sub Shortage Findings:** An analysis of the results of the above survey show that there are significant challenges in finding an adequate number of substitute teachers in Washington, and that the issue is more pronounced in high-need schools.
- **Sub Shortage Leaves Schools Scrambling When Teachers Call In Sick:** With a spotlight on an upstate New York school district, this article from the *Hechinger Report*, a nonprofit news organization focused on innovation and inequality in education, dramatizes the effects of the substitute teacher shortage.
- **Tackling Washington's Teacher Shortage:** This policy brief issued by the governor's office notes that permanent classroom teacher shortages have depleted the pool of substitute teachers. The brief offers solutions for retaining teachers.

- **Wanted: Substitute Teachers. Lots of Them:** The Kent ISD in Michigan offered this window into the effects of a substitute teacher shortage districtwide, and connects this local issue to national trends.

Long-Term Subs

- **Credentialing Commission Considers Slowing Rotation of Substitute Teachers:** The CA Commission on Teacher Credentialing examines whether to extend the amount of time a substitute can be in one classroom in order to meet a growing demand due to increasing numbers of long-term leaves by permanent classroom teachers.

Teacher Absence/Teacher Attendance

- **Frontline: National Employee Absence and Substitute Data:** *Frontline Learning and Research Institute,* a division of *Frontline Education* which produces school administration software, provides monthly and annual reports, and occasional white papers, based on national substitute teacher data.
- **Frontline: Impact of PD on Absences White Paper:** This paper argues that there is a lack of collaboration in managing professionally related absences, which account for a significant percentage of overall teacher absences.
- **Roll Call: The Importance of Teacher Attendance:** This oft-cited paper from the *National Council of Teacher Quality* uses district data from 40 of the nation's largest metropolitan areas to determine how often teachers are in classrooms and what factors influence their attendance.

- **Are Teacher Absences Worth Worrying About in the US?:** Based on data from North Carolina, these researchers find that lower-income students and schools are more adversely affected by teacher absences.
- **Teacher Absence As a Leading Indicator of Student Achievement:** This report from the Center for American Progress examines teacher absence data from the US Department of Education's Office of Civil Rights.
- **Measuring the Effect Teacher Absenteeism Has On Student Achievement at A "Urban but not too urban:" Title I Elementary School:** This journal article concludes that teacher absenteeism can be detrimental to students' education and levels of individual attainment, as measured at a 3rd–6th grade elementary school.

First-Person Reflections

- **Yelling, Crying, and Hugging: All in a (Sub) Day's Work:** A longtime middle-school physical education sub in Michigan shares his experiences.
- Baker, Nicholson. *Substitute: Going to School with A Thousand Kids*. New York: Penguin Press, 2016. Print.
- **Substitute:** In this video, award-winning author Nicholson Baker reads from his book that chronicles the 28 days he spent as a substitute teacher in Maine.

Dissertations

- **Examining Opinions and Perceptions Regarding Substitute Teachers and Their Impact on Student Learning:** This paper focuses on research done at an independent school in which substitute teachers were integrated into the overall school culture.
- **Substitute Teachers As Effective Classroom Instructors:** This oft-cited paper examines issues of professional development for substitute teachers and makes recommendations on how best to support subs in their professional learning.
- **The Impact of Teacher Absenteeism on Student Performance:** The Case of the Cobb County School District: Higher teacher absenteeism leads to lower student math scores on standardized tests in this study, which also found that students attending low-socioeconomic area schools scored significantly lower in reading and math.

Literature Reviews

- **Investigating the Impact of Substitute Teachers on Student Achievement: A Review of Literature:** This research brief attempts to answer the question, "What is the impact of substitute teachers on student achievement?," and provides a set of recommendations to improve their effectiveness.

Books Referenced

Martin, Roger, and Sally Osberg. *Getting Beyond Better: How Social Entrepreneurship Works*

Allard, Harry, and James Marshall. *Miss Nelson Is Missing*

St Michel, Terrie. *Effective Substitute Teachers: Myth, Mayhem or Magic (Roadmap to Success)*. Out of print.

Pink, Daniel. *Drive: The Surprising Truth About What Motivates Us*

Hagan, Margaret, and Kusat Ozence. *Rituals for Work: 50 Ways to Create Engagement, Shared Purpose, and a Culture that Can Adapt to Change*

Vialet, Jill. *Recess Rules*

Acknowledgments

This book is essentially a compilation of a lot of other people's stories, and we are profoundly grateful to them for allowing us to share them with you. Thanks are in order to Jay Midwood, Sarah Cherry Rice, Celeste Huizar, Todd Berman, John Henning, Marquis Taylor, Mike Teng, Carol Zink, Karen DeMoss, Justin Davis, Jeanna Perry, and Traci Taylor. We also want to thank our partners who let us learn alongside them: Cheryl Cotton, Matt Duffy, Amaris Johnson, Michael Gallagher, Megan Burnham, Iris Sanchez, Laura Kaiser, Mindy Feldbaum, Riley Collins, and Charlie Shryock.

The writing process itself is an incredible opportunity for learning and we are especially grateful to Camie Bontaites who has worked as our developmental editor/book midwife, Eliza Wee for her incredible skill and vision with the book layout and design, and Abby VanMuijen for providing the illustrations that amplify the narrative and not infrequently tell our story better than we could ourselves. We are deeply appreciative of Susie Wise for agreeing to write the foreword. Many thanks to Riley Harding from Wiley/ Jossey-Bass who has been an advocate for the book throughout. Margaret Hagan and Kursat Ozenc's book *Rituals for Work* provided design inspiration, and Margaret was a reassuring voice more than once in the process, confirming that what we wanted was possible. Thanks, too, to the folks at the Center for the Collaborative Classroom for sharing your lesson on the class meeting.

We are indebted to many people for the very fact of Substantial—Cristin Quealy, to whom this book is dedicated, was the human who brought so many of our ideas to life. We are also appreciative of the Aspen-Pahara fellowship, where the idea for Substantial first got baked (a special early-believer high five to Simmons Lettre); to Anne Wintroub, Sandro Olivieri, and Amy Mandrier from the AT&T Accelerator for helping us navigate the sometimes confounding waters of edtech; to Holen Robie for holding the fort down while we were writing; and to everyone at Playworks who provided the back office support that Substantial needed. We are also especially indebted to James

Jensen and Kim Tanner of the Jenesis Group for the support that made the whole thing possible. We are amazingly lucky to have such incredible partners in this work.

Lots of humans from the d.school had an influence in the conception of both Substantial the organization and Substantial the book. Susie Wise gets a second helping of thanks here along with Thomas Both, Nadia Roumani, Justin Ferrell, Sarah Stein Greenberg, Devon Young, Ariel Raz, Seamus Yu Harte, and Jen Goldstein. A special shout out to Jill's fellow Fellows: Ashanti Branch, Will Byrne, Patrick Cook-Deegan, Lauren Hancock, Rita Nguyen, and Chris Rudd.

A special thank you to Lynnette Calvin-Epps, who graciously invited Amanda into her work during the sub improvement project. Your moral authority, commitment to the children of Oakland, and willingness to take a relative newbie under your wing continue to be a source of inspiration. Thanks also to Laura Moran and Jill Schiager who provided unwavering support and guidance on that and many other projects. The right mentor at the right time makes all the difference, thanks to Max Silverman, Gee Kin Chou, and Elizabeth Cushing for being that for Amanda.

Finally, we are grateful for the care and persisting good humor of our respective families. Amanda's husband Brian and Jill's partner Elizabeth have been supportive and remarkably good-natured about picking up the slack when the book interfered with normal family operations. Our kids—Penny and Jackson (Amanda) and Caitlin, Koby, Hayden, Walker, and Anders (Jill)—have been our most important guides in understanding education and in constantly reminding us about the most important thing: love.

About the Authors

Jill Vialet

Jill grew up in Washington, DC, attended Harvard University, and spent a year at the Harvard Graduate School of Education where she did her student teaching at Cambridge Rindge and Latin High School. Jill is a serial social entrepreneur, launching the Museum of Children's Art (MOCHA) in 1988 and Playworks in 1996. Jill began working on Substantial initially while an Aspen-Pahara Fellow and took the work to the next level during her year-long fellowship at Stanford's Hasso Plattner Institute of Design (better known as the d.school). Jill is also the co-founder of Workswell, the author of the middle grade novel *Recess Rules*, and an Ashoka fellow. She lives in Oakland, California with her partner Elizabeth with whom she is in various stages of loving and raising five amazing humans.

Amanda von Moos

Amanda von Moos grew up in Chico, California and attended the University of California Santa Cruz. She later received her Masters in Public Policy from UC Berkeley. For the past 15 years Amanda has worked in various capacities to redesign the systems that support schools, as an internal staff member leading process redesign projects in Oakland Unified School District (where among other projects, she helped improve the substitute teacher fill rate), as a program designer and consultant at Pivot Learning Partners, and as the founder of The Central Office Project. As co-founder at Substantial, Amanda brings a passionate commitment to improving the experience of substitute teaching. Amanda lives in Berkeley, California with her husband Brian and their two children.

Index